LIFE WISDOM: IMPORTANT LESSONS I HOPE MY CHILDREN WOULD LEARN

Path to Riches, Freedom and Happiness

Phil N. Jonathan

Phil N. Jonathan

For Eleanor... and for all who will live with Eleanor...

CONTENTS

INTRODUCTION

I hope all of the people in the world are happy because I believe happy people make others become happy and it will make the world a better place in which to live. And also because I wish that my daughter will always be happy and surrounded by happy people. To contribute to that, I would like to help as many as people to know 'WHAT IT IS', 'HOW TO BE', and 'WHAT TO DO' for their happiness through this book.

You have your own mission given by heaven. And you have 4 periods in your life.

I. To have body, personality, and intelligence that are necessary to carry out your mission.

II. To create your own philosophy that can make you accurately understand and follow your mission.

III. To satisfy your mission by carrying it out.

IV. To make up for the parts that were lacking during the mission and look back on life.

I hope you follow and carry out the advice I will explain in this book, especially in the first and second periods of your life. Then, I'm sure that you will become a great philosopher and will be moving toward continuous happiness without any regrets later in your life time.

I tried my best to build the concept and formula as much as

possible to be universal and error free in this book. Nevertheless, you may find some content that is contradictory and difficult to generalize due to the changes of time or generalization fallacy. Even so, I believe there would be no difficulty in establishing or enlightening the philosophy to help you lead a happy life.

In this book, I will further explain the parts one dealing with the concept and theory and the other dealing with ways of practice. Understanding concepts alone can't make changes and executing without understanding can greatly reduce the efficiency. Therefore, I hope you understand the concepts carefully even though they would be boring and difficult, and execute them in the right direction based on correct understanding.

Then, let's take the first step toward making a happy life from now on.

PROLOGUE

Desperation

[An e-mail has arrived.]

I finally felt relief thinking, 'Phew, fortunately I got the reply. I can reply to the customer now,' and write and send an email about an urgent issue that has been overdue. And I wake up. It was a dream about receiving the email I had been waiting for.

When I go to work and check my messy email inbox, I find many emails that I need to reply to. I wonder thinking, 'Huh? I thought I already replied to them,' and I check my sent items, but I can't find any emails that I replied to.

For some time I have been working every night in my dreams. I can't tell dreams from reality. Even after work, I'm very anxious about work, and the quality of my life seems to have gone down.

I thought something was wrong. It is certainly a weird symptom that the boundary between dreams and reality is not clear. I got various tests done and had a consultation in a neuropsychiatry hospital and I was found to have early symptoms of depression. I thought I was under a lot of stress, but I never thought that I was depressed.

Looking back on my life, it was quite successful without that many difficulties. I kept my academic grades up and went to a quite good university. After graduating from university, I was appointed as a naval officer. I received a relatively sizable salary at a tender age and the pension was guaranteed. However, I didn't have much fun with army life and thought my freedom was greatly limited. So I got discharged from the army. Acquaintances including family and relatives were very opposed to this and were disappointed in my decision, but I was ok. I was confident that I could have a better life.

After leaving the army, I traveled abroad. As I freely traveled as I wanted without any restrictions or limitations, I felt like my life was pretty cool. But as the money I had saved started to run low, I felt financial anxiety. So I prepared for a job and eventually joined a major global company. My parents were very proud of me and my relatives and friends congratulated me. I could have more freedom in a general company than the army and I felt that my life was finally perfectly balanced.

From childhood I vaguely thought that I would be rich in the future. My salary wasn't that low compared to other industries except for specific high-paying jobs or industries. I belonged to the top 20% of the salary ranking reported in the news. I thought it was quite good to be in the top 20% being in my early 30s and I thought that I could be rich at any moment. Of course, I might not be able to become a plutocrat, but I believed that I could be rich enough to splurge sometimes without having problems while living because, while working at a stable and competent company, the increasing rate of salary was good and I even prepared a pension savings and various types of insurance.

But now, I was under stress and had depression…. Why did my life that was satisfying and filled with pride suddenly encounter such a big wall? I thought that depression is a symptom that only a few people who have weak willpower or are vulnerable to stress suffer. Since I thought that I had lived successfully and well without any problems so far, I had a fundamental question at this point. *What is the problem? Where did it go wrong?* When I thought about it, I found that it would be because I didn't have money. If I didn't need to worry about money, I could do whatever I want. If I didn't like working at a company, I could just quit, or if I wanted to travel around, I could travel to places I wanted to just because I could.

I watched YouTube today as usual without having any particular thoughts while worrying about work at the company. I didn't have a particular topic of interest. I just played videos that looked interesting from the recommendations list on YouTube. Then, a sudden thought appeared about something and I turned off the video. And then I searched the key phrases: 'How to earn money' and 'How to become rich'.

Change

As I watched YouTube, it seemed that the way to get out of my situation now was investment. I expected that I could quit my job and live comfortably if I could increase my fortune and make cash flow through investment.

I thought I had to invest in real estate to make the cash flow every month. I wanted to quit my job right away and do some investment, but my balance was close to zero. I needed at least $30,000 to invest and it would take at least a few years to save that much. I learned that I should change my life patterns and save the money persistently through a video, but I doubted I could do that. Even if I could, I thought I could only save a few hundred dollars a month after cutting down my spending.

I decided to read books that were mentioned a lot in many videos since saving money is a matter of time. I first read *Rich Dad Poor Dad* by Robert Kiyosaki, which is considered to be the Bible of investment, and indeed, it was as great as its reputation foretold it to be. But I couldn't think of anything special I could do, so I decided to attend investment seminars as the book recommended.

There were many videos that told me about the concept of investment on YouTube. Among them, I tried to search for a video that simply explained about actual investment to make cash flow and induced the application of seminar, and I found it. In particular, the lecturer looked to be sincere. So, the next day, I contacted and applied for the seminar right away. The cost of the seminar was $600 with five sessions for five weeks. I had read that Robert Kiyosaki also participated in the first seminar with a similar price, so I was very curious and excited if I could make a turning point in my life through this.

I learned a lot at the seminar. I learned about the concept of investment and got to know how to invest in the real world. But the big problem here was that I had no money in my account. I realized that when I saved enough money to invest later, the price of assets would have already increase by that time and I would need a larger amount of money for investment. And the earning rate would be lower than it was now.

At the third session of the seminar, I learned something new, that even if the money for an investment is not sufficient, it is possible to invest with a loan. So I inquired a credit loan for office workers and I found that I could borrow about $70,000. Considering an interest rate of 3.9%, the loan rate would be $230 per month. It was quite large, but I thought that I could have about 10-12% of annual earnings with the investment method explained in the seminar. If I could have a 12% earning rate, I could earn about $700 and would earn $470 even after deducting interest.

As I learned about investments through the seminar, my head was filled with the thought of investing as soon as possible and quitting my job. Then one day, an instructor from the seminar contacted me to visit since he had found a good item. I was very excited that I could make the first investment, so I rushed to the place instructor told me to go to, leaving everything behind. When I checked the item in the field, I tried to apply the theory that I had learned at the seminar. But I couldn't remember what I learned well and I couldn't judge whether it was good or bad. I just trusted the instructor and signed a contract right away full of expectations for the investment. The purchase amount was higher than I thought at first, but I had gotten $70,000 from the credit loan and the insufficient amount was made up with a mortgage loan for the contracted item. Consequently, I invested in it 100% with a loan.

After making the first investment, I received the monthly rent for a few months. I felt like my life was finally going as I wanted. However not long after that, the monthly rent started to be unpaid and the tenant didn't answer my calls. Finally when I met and talked with him, he asked me to give him more time since he was having a hard time. Even after that, the tenant continued to fail to pay the rent and I finally asked him to leave. The tenant said okay, but he didn't leave easily and finally left after almost spending his entire deposit. As such, my first investment began with anxiety and the expectation of changing my life through investment in real estate seemed to go wrong. I began to feel more anxious at that time, but my first investment was very successful anyway. Of course, it became clear later, and I had enough hardships and suffering through that investment.

Enlightenment

Apart from the first investment, I continued to search for investment related videos and materials, participate in seminars, and read books. As I read several self-help books, I learned that our lives move in the direction we think. So I left my company. It was a really good company, enough to think that I would work there until retirement, but it wasn't that difficult to make up my mind to quit because I thought I could change jobs based on an 8-year career and I also could bear several months with severance pay. Most of all, I wanted to focus more on studies for investment.

For about 3 months after quitting my job, I went to the library to read books. And if there were good seminars, I participated in them regardless of the topic. Looking back on those days, my first investment became the seed of changes in my life, and the 3 months after quitting my job became the foundation for me to take a big step in a changed direction.

When I read books and attended seminars for 3 months, I found something all successes have in common. I found that successful people are always seen with books and newspapers, trying to learn continuously to turn learning into money making and they have certain lifestyle patterns. After finding these facts, I created my own lifestyle pattern. Even though my balance was rapidly decreasing, I didn't feel worried or anxious because I realized how I should live my life.

New life

I joined a new company. The salary wasn't that high and it was an IT related company, which was totally different from my career. So far, I had taken it for granted to apply for a company that I could receive the highest salary based on my career, but my perspective for working had changed while studying and attending seminars for 3 months.

I estimated that if I worked at this company for 7 more years while following the lifestyle pattern I set, the condition for my first goal would be achieved. My first goal was to live the way I wanted to and to earn twice as much as my current salary as an asset income even without working, as well as to do business and investment, I wanted freedom through this.

But as I actually experienced everything, I realized that my estimation was not accurate. Many successful people said that goals are achieved much faster than expected once the change has begun. And it was true.

My lifestyle pattern became a habit and this habit made me a very positive person. And a positive attitude changed my life dramatically. I felt like the whole world was helping me. The house I purchased after marriage wasn't really worth it at first, but the price increased and I could receive an additional loan through this. The net amount of money I spent to purchase the house was about $160,000, but additional loans available to me with the increase of the house's price exceeded $200,000. With additional loans and my remaining severance pay, I remodeled the first investment and eventually the rate of earning became 17%, and I could do two more investments. I had no need to wait for experts to contact me for the second and third investments because I learned the entire process through the first investment and I already had the necessary skills and personal connections. The opportunity for the second investment came like a miracle as if attracted by a magnet. When I was on the site for remodeling of the first invested item, I was able to meet the seller. The other opportunity for investment also came when I was with a real estate agent and accidently connected with the seller. Of course, there were variables and difficulties in the new investments, but I could fully cope with them. During a series of these processes, the cash flow that was created was worth more than my salary.

Once my assets increased and cash flow was created, the speed at which the investment money was saved became faster. And the limit for getting loans had also increased. I did investment and purchased estates, gold, and silver with the saved and borrowed money. Through my personal connections which expanded during my investments, my cash flow increased again with investment in other things than real estate. Finally, my first goal was achieved in about 1.5 years, not 7 years.

My new life, which went through these processes, completely broke out of the slump of desperation I experienced when I was in my first job. Of course, I had big and small losses due to excessive desire or wrong judgment, but I was becoming stable. This is because I was convinced that the asset structure I created would not be easily broken and even if it was a little bit broken, I believed I could recover it without difficulty as long as I continuously kept my lifestyle pattern. So, I could move toward new goals while freely doing business and investments as I wanted.

* * *

Here, I would like to summarize my pleasant experiences and what I've learned. If you need some changes in your life and hope for this, I hope you can read this book and try to practice what I did. Then, I'm sure you can change your life dramatically.

PART I. LIFE

I'm a philosopher. I love to explore essence and wisdom. Since I lived as a philosopher, I've been in the path of happiness.

Just like most of the parents around me, my parents also took a lot of care in my education and career since I was very young. When I came home after school, they asked me what I learned and what was difficult that day, and they gave me direct supplementary studying to do. Getting good academic grades was the best pleasure for my parents and they hoped that I would join a reputational company or get a job like a judge or doctor in the future.

My parents are not rich. The economic education I got from them can be summarized as, "Don't be greedy," "If you work hard, money will naturally come along," "If you save money, you will certainly be rich," "You should thoroughly prepare for the elderly years with pension plans," "Do not invest in stocks," and "Do not stand surety for anyone."

I wasn't interested in studying when I was in school. I enjoyed reading comic books or playing games and I wanted to learn musical instruments and date rather than studying. However I felt it was a sin not to study, so I spent most of the time studying with uncertain concentration as I wasn't interested in it. I thought I could do well if I worked hard, but 'working hard' didn't work. My grades were so ordinary, closer to the upper level rather than the lower level, but there was nothing I had confidence in, so I was without any particular hobbies or specialties.

I thought a lot about how to choose my career. I couldn't figure out what I really wanted to do and what I could do well. So,

I just focused on what was given to me every day. I decided to be a soldier who doesn't have to worry about the future and went to a military school. I didn't have a special sense of duty, but it seemed that a certain degree of a sense of duty had naturally been made as I received education and training.

Life as a soldier was simple. There weren't any big problems if I only did my job and followed what I was ordered to do, but I could imagine what my future would be like, the future where I would be promoted when the time came, and if I couldn't be recognized for a special achievement, I would be promoted to some extent and then discharged from the army in time. So, it wasn't fun. What would it mean even if I worked hard and rose to a higher position without having fun? If I lived according to the fixed rules, retired when I got older and lived in my old age with a set amount of pension to sustain life, what meaning could I give to my existence? 'Working hard' didn't work at the army.

I really wanted to do my best at a company I newly enjoyed. I wanted to find the reward and pleasure in the work and try hard to be recognized. The company said that sales were about selling values, not goods. I couldn't understand what the value of the goods I was selling was, but I tried my best to sell the value to the customers. So, I studied the various technologies and explained a lot of them to the customers. It seemed that the customers were satisfied with that approach. As I approached while considering the value, the contract was concluded when I could meet the desired price of the customers and the contract failed when the price wasn't matched. Nevertheless, the company praised me for doing well and I thought I was following well what company wished. But I didn't know if I was really doing well, I didn't know what the value was, and most of all, it wasn't fun. Perhaps this was why 'working hard' at the company didn't work.

I became a philosopher in search of answers to continuous and connected questions such as 'Why can't I do anything hard?', 'Why do I think I have to do something hard?', 'What does it mean to work hard?', 'What do I really want?', 'How do I want to live?', 'Why am I living?', 'What about my value?', and 'What about my existence?'

CHAPTER 1. THE FOUNDATION OF LIVING WELL

Anyone would have thought of 'I want to live well'. What does it mean to live well? To find the answer for this question, we need to have an insight into life itself.

Just like two sides of the same coin, there is always the other side of death in life. Therefore, life is a subject that should be dealt with death. Then, why are we alive at this moment? It is because we chose life between life and death.

If I say it like this, there would be many people who would raise an objection saying, 'Death is not something we can choose'. But think about this, that many people in the world chose death for themselves. People who are in extreme conditions or who are suffering from very painful illnesses choose to die to escape from their current situation or pain. There were even ancient philosophers who recognized life itself as pain and encouraged people to die to be free from it. In addition, there would be people who choose to die for various reasons such as a supreme sacrifice or due to unavoidable choices. Anyway, from the point of view of possible and impossible, not right and wrong, man clearly can choose death by themselves and the reason we are living at this moment is because we chose life.

Then, why do we choose life? It would be quite difficult to explain the answer clearly, but one of the reasons might be because of the fear of death. Everyone has the fear of death. It would be fear for the pain that might inevitably accompany the process of death or it would be vague fear of the unknown world which we never experienced. Or there may be a sense of guilt or sorrow for the loss of relations.

However, if we take some time for introspection through philosophers and thinkers or religions, the fear of death would not come to a great extent. According to *Phaedon* by Plato, Socrates told the following stories to his friends who tried to save him in the face of death.

"We can't get true knowledge through the sense of flesh. We can get true knowledge only through pure thought and reasoning. But pure thoughts and reasoning are only available in the state where the soul is completed free from the body, that is, deadness. Therefore, death for philosophers who seek true knowledge is rather pursuit and aspiration."

This means that death is not an object of pain and fear, but rather an object of pursuit and aspiration. Epicurus, another ancient philosopher said the following:

"As long as we exist, death doesn't stay with us, and when death comes, we no longer exist. Then, death has nothing to do with the living or the dead. It is because death has not come yet for the living and the dead do not already exist."

In addition to these, if we take some time for introspection with numerous philosophies, ideas, and religions, the fear of death might nearly fade away. Of course, it would be still difficult or even impossible to be completely free from the fear of death.

What I'm trying to say is that from the point of view of choice, you have to decrease the fear of death and place life and death in an equal position. Indeed, if we are at the crossroads between life and death, fear would not be the decisive factor for choice. While there is fear in death, there is suffering in life. There is no way to completely eliminate it. That is, if there is a reason for difficulties in choosing death, there would be factors that make the choice difficult in choosing life, too.

Because there are difficulties in making the choice for both life and death, the choice may be determined according to some factors. The reason for choosing life between life and death is not because it is easier, but because it is better. If we look around, we can see some people saying, "I just live because I can't die," or "I don't like to live, but I can't die because of the fear," but it's not good to think like that. It was just because those people didn't have a deep introspection about life or death and that they just couldn't find good things in life or didn't even try to find them. I'm sure that if we give those people enough money to live without worrying about living their lives, most of them would immediately be filled with the willingness to live in the world happily. The reason we are living in this world at this moment is because we chose our own lives and feel that life is better than death.

Then, let's ask ourselves the question again. Why am I living? It would be difficult to have the perfect answer for this, but 'happiness' is probably the biggest reason. It means that we choose life because our lives at this moment are happy, or at least there is hope to be happy in the future, or because of the desire to be happy. All the acts we are making such as working hard in an organization, trying to earn a lot of money, trying to be recognized as a good member of society, and trying to love or being loved by someone are ultimately to feel happy.

If it's true that we chose life between life and death and the reason is happiness, then it means that living well is living happily. And when we look at the life as a whole, if you have more happy times, you are living well, and if you have less happy times, you are not living well.

Happiness

We have to live happily to live well. To live happily, we first need to understand what happiness is. It is difficult to define happiness simply, but at least we all know happiness is an emotional state and belongs to the realm of feeling anyway. We feel happy when we are doing what we want to do. We feel happy when we are eating what we want to eat, doing what we want to do, enjoying what we want to enjoy, and when we love someone we want to love. The important thing here is that we feel happiness 'when we are doing' what we want to do, not 'after doing something' that we want to do.

Some people may think that 'satisfaction' and 'happiness' are the same feeling, but these two are totally different. We feel happiness when we are doing what we want to do and feel satisfaction after doing something we want to do. For example, we want to eat something when we are very hungry. And we feel happy when we are eating and feel satisfaction after eating. Aristotle also mentioned the same content as *"Happiness is not gained in the future, but is in the process."*

When we look at the whole process of solving one's desires, it leads to 'deficiency → desire → dissolution → satisfaction'. The stage of feeling happiness here is the stage of dissolution. When we are very hungry, we have a deficiency of hunger, we have desire to eat something to escape from the deficiency, we dissolve the desire in the process of eating something and feel happiness, and then we feel satisfaction after completely dissolving the desire. Once again, we feel happiness when we are eating and feel satisfaction after eating since our hunger disappears. Of course, deficiency and desire occur complexly in most cases, just like we have desire to eat certain foods in a certain place, but I used a very simple example for easy understanding here.

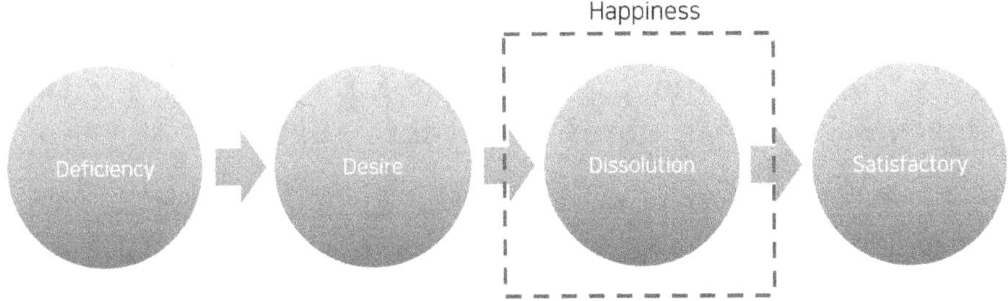

Another important thing is that happiness is a sense that can be obtained in the process of continuously dissolving desires, not a destination or object that can be reached by achieving certain goals once. If you clearly understand this point, you may know that sayings like "If I become rich, I will live happily forever," or "If I have a good job, I will be happy," come from a misconception.

If you read this writing carefully so far, you may able to infer how to live your life happily: it is to live continuously finding your deficiencies and dissolving desires caused by them. Everyone will feel certain deficiencies and have desires that come from them. Therefore, if you recognize and accept your deficiencies well, there would be more chances to feel greater happiness. Great saints such as Sakyamuni and Chuang-tze have suggested a way to live well by controlling ourselves so that desire itself is not made, but I will leave it out of my discussion since it is beyond the scope of what I can deal with. From the point of view I suggested, satisfying the present life by riding our greed and lowering our standards is not a happy and good life. Living by actively dissolving our desires and feeling greater happiness is a good life. For this, you need a system that can increase the amount of happiness as much as possible. The system I suggest is to lay aside the largest desires that are difficult to completely dissolve in a lifetime, then place desires that need to be dissolved over a long time, and finally place fragmentary desires on them. The desires that can't be completed dissolved in a lifetime are a mission and desires that need to be dissolved over a long time are visions. Fragmentary desires are literally the ones in every moment you experience in your daily life, like hunger. I will explain more in detail on mission and vision later.

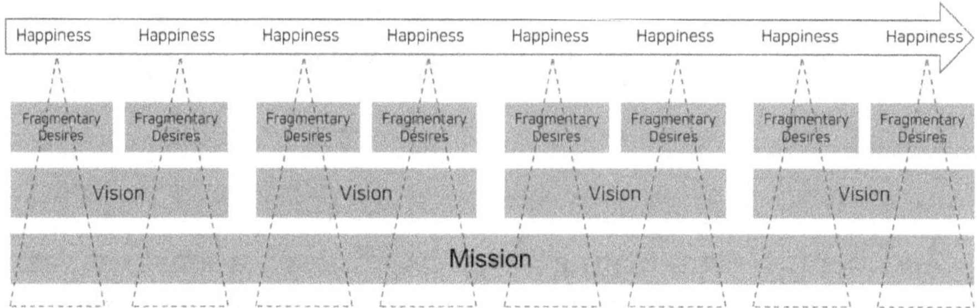

Freedom

You should pursue happiness to live your life well. To do this, freedom is inevitably required. Freedom to do actual acts to dissolve your desires such as the freedom to have and eat what you want to eat, the freedom to go where you want to go, and the freedom to do what you want to do is essential. Now, let's look how to obtain and enjoy freedom.

Freedom is control. It means that if there is freedom, there is also control, and if freedom is exercised, control is also exercised. Being free from certain domains means we can freely exercise control over that domain according to our will. For example, being free from physical activity means we can act according to our will by controlling our bodies. On the contrary, if we lose control due to a physical defect or disability, it means that the freedom of that part is limited. In detail, prisoners may have freedom of their body itself, but they lose control over social activities, having no freedom to move in places or do activities at certain timed that they want to. In this context, having strong control over one's own self means being freer from one's physical and mental longings or habits.

Control comes from possession. Being able to fully exercise control over an object means we completely possess it. We can use our own items freely because our own items here means we have complete ownership of them. For example, if the house you live in is owned under your name only without any mortgage loan, you can freely do anything such as decorating, remodeling, lending, or selling the house. On the other hand, if the house is owned under a joint name, you can't do anything freely without the consent of the other owner, and if the house is lent to a tenant, the ownership of the house is limited during that period and you can't exercise control over it. And if there is a mortgage loan for the house, the lender may hand over the house to auction depending on the circumstances. That is, control is not fully exercised if ownership is not complete.

Freedom is often divided into financial freedom and temporal freedom, but I don't think it is necessary to distinguish these two. Freedom depends on whether ownership can be obtained regardless of if it is financial freedom or temporal freedom because both of these can be obtained by money.

Financial freedom is obtained when the ownership of the object which is intended to exercise control is obtained. To exercise control, that is, to enjoy freedom, we need to acquire ownership first and we need to pay an appropriate amount of money for that. Having financial freedom means having as much as money we need.

Ownership also exists in time. Time is given equally to everyone, but the freedom to be enjoyed by people who have complete ownership of time and those who don't have it are different. We can often see people saying, "I have money, but I don't have time to spend it." It is probably because they need to work. People who work at a company normally have a contract to work for 8 hours a day. The 8 contracted hours are owned by the company. Since they lose the ownership of about 10 hours including commute time out of the 24 hours in a day, they can't enjoy temporal freedom. Even in this case, if there is no economic problem, they can regain the ownership of time by terminating or cancelling their contract. In other words, ownership of time can be obtained with money. Therefore, having temporal freedom means having as much money as we need as well.

With these reasons, I say ownership can be obtained with money, and the more money you have, the more freedom you can enjoy.

One thing to keep in mind is that when you obtain ownership with money and have control over something, you should exercise it well. Having freedom and enjoying freedom are different. There is no infinite freedom in reality. This is because there are various restrictions and limitations such as physical restrictions, legal restrictions, moral restrictions, and willpower limitations. Therefore, if you gain ownership and control over a certain object, you should enjoy freedom within the restrictions and limitations of control. Just like we don't give dangerous objects to kids who lack control, the world doesn't grant ownership to those who can't properly exercise control. And sometimes it takes back ownership of what they already have. Moving and acting thoroughly within the boundaries of the law based on ethics and morality is the way to keep one's control, that is, freedom.

Riches

The last piece we need to live our lives well is riches, that is money. People often say like, "Money is not everything," or "Having a lot of money doesn't mean being happy." This is half right and half wrong. Having a lot of money doesn't mean being happy, but we obviously need money to be happy. As I said, you should find your deficiencies and dissolve the desires that come from them to be happy. You need freedom to dissolve desires and freedom begins with the acquisition of ownership, meaning having as much money as you need. So you need money for the happiness you are pursuing at this moment.

You need to be rich to live your life well, that is, to live happily. Rich refers to those who have a lot of money. At this point, you need to understand about the criteria of having a lot of money. You can't distinguish between those who are rich and those who are not with only their amount of money. The rich are those who know their own desires and have enough money to obtain freedom for dissolving them. If some already have as much money as they need to be rich, those who have large-sized desires are richer and those who have small-sized desires are less rich.

Everyone may want to be rich. For that, you need to accurately recognize its purpose and method. It is that you need to accumulate riches to be happy, not just making money to be rich. It means that you should look at riches from the point of view of happiness. Some people say that, "Money naturally follows if you do your best at your position." I won't say this is totally wrong, but it's a bit different. You shouldn't consider this as a way to be rich.

If you just work hard for the purpose of work itself, money corresponding to the amount of work will naturally follow along, but it is a completely different matter than being rich. The money that comes along when you understand your deficiencies and desires and pursue happiness will make you rich. If you don't understand your deficiencies and desires, you won't know the amount of riches you need to be free, and you will never be rich accordingly.

Not understanding their own deficiencies and desires is why many people who look rich in reality are actually fake rich. For fake rich people, it is difficult for them to maintain their great riches even if they obtained them through successful business, investments, etc. In the case of fake rich people who gained great riches by inheritance or lottery, their riches might disappear more quickly. You may often see the story of people who gained a lot of money with the lottery, but spent all of it in a short amount of time and became homeless. This is because they just pursued money itself. Real rich people pursuing happiness dissolve their current desires. They become richer by constantly pursuing happiness in a way that find suitable and dissolve their other deficiencies and desires after their current ones are satisfied. As the more noble and humble people know about themselves and the world, the more they realize there's a greater shortage, that is, deficiency. So, rich people are always humble and try to find their own deficiencies and desires. In this way, real rich people gain more happiness and make greater riches.

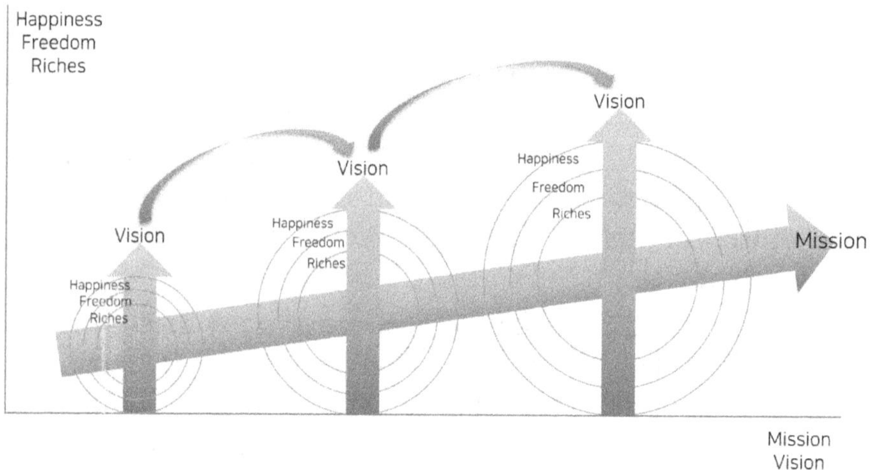

* * *

As such, we have looked at the basic concepts we should have to live well. The way to live well is to find our deficiencies, accept them as they are, and dissolve desires that come from such processes while pursuing happiness. If we move in the right direction for gaining happiness, freedom and riches will naturally follow.

CHAPTER 2. THE IMPORTANT FACTORS IN LIFE

To live well, you must know not only yourself, but also various factors such as the structure, laws, and interactions of the world. Let's look at some of the factors that connect the foundation of life which are happiness, freedom, and riches.

Mission

To have a system that maximizes the size of happiness in your life, you first need to place desires that can't be completely dissolved in your lifetime, then place desires that need to be dissolved over a long period of time on top of them, and lastly place fragmentary desires over them. Desire that can't be completely dissolved is a mission and the one that needs to be dissolved over a long period of time is a vision.

When humans are born, they are commanded by heaven about what role they will play in the world to live. This is called a mission, and a mission is a guideline from heaven about the value the human must provide to the world.

Because it's the command from heaven, you must live while fulfilling your mission from heaven throughout your lifetime. If you work at a company, you continuously receive work to do from the company and such work never ends even after you leave the company, rather someone else takes it over. For students, studying never ends. This is because they can never study all of the things in the world. So, I can say work at a company or studying are given in the form of deficiencies that can't be completely filled. If you fill the deficiencies while working or studying, there would be a sense of achievement. Meaning, you would be happy. In opposing cases, you might feel anxiety and sometimes even guilt. It works same for the mission given to one's life. And the degree of happiness that comes from fulfilling the given mission and anxiety that comes from not fulfilling it would be incomparable to the degree from work or studying. Therefore, you must always try to fulfill your mission while living and that is the way to live with lifelong happiness.

If you understand your mission, you can clearly know the direction of your life. People often say that direction is more important than speed. It is a mission that outlines the direction of life. Once again, a mission can never be completed in a lifetime. And heaven doesn't command us to complete our missions, but just outlines their directions. The mission of Amazon is "to serve consumers through online and physical stores and focus on selection, price, and convenience". The mission of Facebook is "to give people the power to build community and bring the world closer together". The mission of the apostle Paul in the Bible might be "to preach the gospel to all the people in the world". The missions mentioned above can never be completed and they only outline directions. As such, if you are able to figure out your missions, you will know how to live your life and what values you will provide to the world. And that direction will lead you to the way of happiness.

At this point, you may have one question that how you can know your mission. If you can directly receive a divine revelation from God or an angel like the apostle Paul or Mohammed, you would know your mission right away. However it is really unusual and it would be almost impossible to expect to have the same experience in your life. It is said that Confucius got to know his mission at age 50 and Socrates discovered his mission in the middle of his life. It is also said that Genghis Khan began to carry out his mission when he ascended the position of Great Khan at age 51. As we might know from the above cases, it can take a long time to know your mission and, maybe, most people will live without ever even knowing their missions in their lifetime.

Therefore, you need to make special effort to find your mission. The way I suggest is to listen carefully to yourself as much as possible and know yourself well, then to set your mission first. To set your mission, it would be good to find something in which the three factors of 'what I do well', 'what do I like', and 'what is worthy to make money' can be commonly applied. When heaven grants a mission to someone, it also gives them appropriate talent. If you find something you are good at and if your will and the will of heaven match, you can enjoy yourself and heaven will also help you. And if you gain recognition for the value of your mission, it will lead to money. When you regularly check and adjust your mission set in this way, the mission you set will get closer to the true mission granted by heaven. Just as "Heaven helps those who help themselves," it will surely tell the true mission to those who are constantly trying to find their missions.

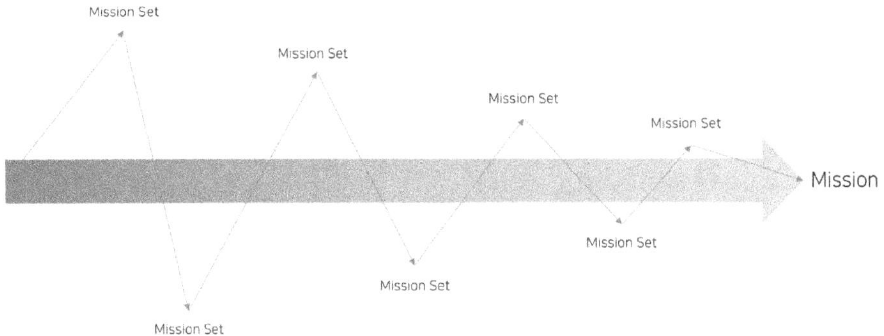

Vision

Unlike a mission that can't be completely fulfilled in a lifetime, vision is the one that should be fulfilled. Vision is to set a direction so that you can fulfill your mission. So, when your mission is clearer, it is easier to set a vision. When your vision is fulfilled, the deficiencies of your mission can also be equally fulfilled, and as you move toward a greater vision in the next step, greater amounts of deficiencies of your mission can be fulfilled. While a mission tells you the direction of your life, a vision can be a milestone in your life. Through this, you would be able to measure how much of your mission you have fulfilled.

Vision can be set with a clear goal over a medium to long term such as 5-year, 10-year, or 20-year period, and short-term plans and daily routines can be cleared depending on the vision. And you can know the value you must have through your vision. This is the same as the process necessarily accompanying the establishment and growth of a company. It is to understand the mission, set the vision, make a short-term plan accordingly, and have needed core values. And it is surely more important for you to do the process much more elaborately than what a company does.

Value

It is crucial to understand values because values are the criteria for all comparison and judgment in your life. In addition, the process of creating values must be treated as very important since it is the same as the process of living according to the mission and the vision.

The nature of value is an impression which is an energy effecting people's mind in positive ways such as joy, pleasure, comfort, and peace. Let's take delicious food as an example. The food provides values like taste and energy to people. People obtain pleasure through sweet or sour tastes and textures and get a feeling of satiety. People also get the opportunity to act and think through the energy the food provides. That means that the food provided values to people and their minds moved in a positive direction. If the food is rotten and results in a stomach ache, or is not tasty and made them disappointed, they would not gain an impression and even have a negative feeling. As a result, it would make it difficult for people to feel the value of food. As another example, since means of transportation provides positive value to users through comfort, convenience, and speed, people use transportation. Purchasing goods or service is also an act that occurs when people's minds move in a positive direction.

You can exchange value. Purchasing and selling goods and services is an exchange of value. From the point of view of purchasing, it is to provide value in the medium of money, and from the point of view of selling, it is to give the values of goods or services. And the values can meet other values to create new values or grow together. For example, when the value of land and the value of labor force come together, agricultural products are produced and they provide new value to people. For another example, when value given by land, by buildings, by transportation, and by service meet and form, the market and the values grow together in the form of a commercial district.

All values consist of matter and adhesive. In the matters mentioned here, there is an element, the smallest physical unit of an object, and there is naturality that has no substance, but constitutes certain objects such as time, space, and spirit. Matter itself has its own value and contributes to new values created by combining with other values. Adhesive refers to a mental ability such as imagination or creativity. I will refer to it as imagination here. Imagination itself also has its own value and creates a new unit of value by combining with other values. Most values take the form of a combination of matter and imagination. Here, I will divide it into and refer to it as 'matter', 'imagination', and the combination of matter and imagination as a 'material' of value. Almost all the values we encounter in reality take the form of combination of material (matter + imagination) and imagination. The combination of material and imagination becomes one new material unit and it again becomes a new material unit by combining with another imagination.

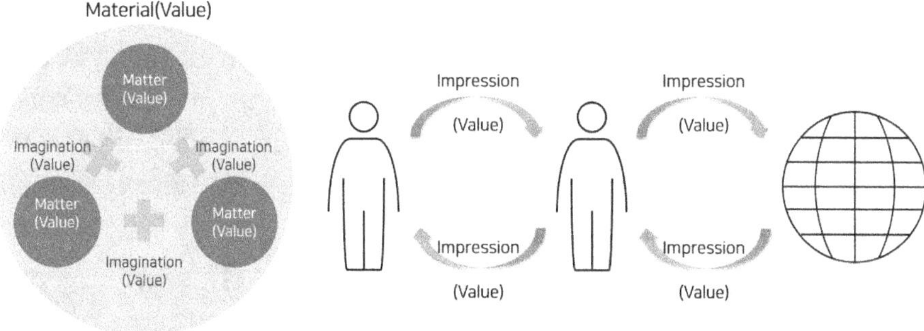

Let's break down one value material to help you understand better. If imagination is removed from an automobile, it will break down into materials such as an engine, gear, wheels, exterior materials, and interior materials. Again, if imagination is removed from the engine, it will break down into materials such as a cylinder, valve, piston, and bolt. Once again, if imagination is removed from the bolt, it will break down into a chunk of various types of metallic elements. Through the process of breaking things down, you can see that one new value material is created when materials (or sometimes matters only) are combined with imagination.

At this point, you need to consider the ratio between the matter and imagination of value. Metals such as gold and silver themselves provide impressions to people like stability and pleasure, that is, a value. In this case, matter takes 100% of the value of gold and silver. Time and space provide the value of opportunity to people. Opportunity here means the one in which imagination can be exercised. Pure time and space themselves don't contain imagination and matter takes 100% in the ratio of value. At this point, pure time and space with no imagination don't have great value and when imagination is combined, a great value is created. Therefore, the time and space of people who don't use their imagination have almost no value. Conversely, for people who have good imagination, time and space have great value. On the other hand, when it comes to social institutions, financial systems, or company organizations, imagination takes almost 100% in the ratio of value. What you can know here is that if the material of value is more natural and physical, the value ratio of matter will be higher, and if it is not, the value ratio of imagination will be higher. Since this can be an important clue for comparing and judging values, you need to fully understand it.

The value of matter never disappears, but the value of imagination has its lifespan. In other words, the value of matter will be eternal, but the value of imagination will depreciate. For example, the value of the space itself occupied by a house is eternal, but buildings or interiors, which consist mostly of the portion of imagination, gradually depreciate over time. However there are some exceptions. In case of some works of art, imagination takes most of the value ratio, but the material itself takes the form of one matter. In this case depreciation does not occur.

It is an imagination that grows value and normally takes much more than matter in the size of value. Matter itself can't grow value by itself. You may easily understand if you think about goods such as automobiles, smartphones, or houses. In this case, the value of imagination is far greater than the value of matters, and it's imagination that explosively grows value of objects.

Lastly, let's analyze the value of people. Ever since people are born, they already have energy that gives impression, that is, value. The matters naturally given to people are a 'spirit' and an 'ability' itself to exercise imagination. People are loved because they have a spirit. The spirit of newborn babies provides parents or foster parents the value of joy, and parents and foster parents repay the value received from the spirit of babies with love.

Since everyone's spirit has a value and gives it to the world, the world repays people with other values. And all the people create the value received from the world into new valuable materials through imagination. As such, people provide value to the world and receive new value in return to grow values. In this way, values circulate through the world and the people. Remember again that people have 'spirit' and 'ability' for imagination which are matters, the minimum unit of values. Therefore, the existence of humans is always valuable and has the power to grow value.

Asset

Asset is a container to put value in. Asset and value are fundamentally different concepts, but since asset generally contains value, I will refer to the container that contains value as asset. Asset is a means of storing the values accumulated while living according to your mission and vision. It is also an essential tool for acquiring riches to be happy. Therefore, it is very important to understand features such as what kind of values the asset contains and what the ratio of the matter and imagination of the value is. There are many forms in asset such as people, money, real estate, stocks, bonds, establishments, raw materials, and works of art, and it also has its own nature. You may be able to easily understand what I mean by looking at some examples of important asset types as the following.

1)   Human

Humans already have a 'spirit' and 'ability' for imagination, it means that humans contain values and let's say those are primary matters of humans. Humans store additional values received from outside as materials such as knowledge and experience. And humans combine these materials with imagination to create new values. In the values additionally stored in humans other than primary matters, imagination takes 100% of them, and its value is being depreciated. Depreciation appears as loss due to either oblivion or imagination becoming outdated and difficult to apply. On the other hand, imagination does not take physical space, so the amount of value which humans can store is infinite. Therefore, you need to continuously accept the value and exercise imagination to grow the value. This means that the amount of value to grow must be larger than the amount of value that is depreciated. Since human activity itself is a process of accepting values from outside and exercising the imagination, the amount of value tends to increase without making any special effort. However, it is totally different between letting value grow by itself and actively growing value. So, it is natural that value grows much more when you try harder.

2)   Money

Money contains the value of convenience, standard of exchange, and credit from the government; it means money contains 100% imagination. It is not possible for additional values to be combined and the only way to grow the value of money is to improve the government's credit rating.

The numbers shown on money create the standard for the exchange of value, and most exchanges of value are made with money. Since money is used when actually exchanging the value, people often understand that the value of money is equal to the size of exchangeable value. This is because people tend to evaluate value with the numbers shown on money. In fact, the total size of values in the world continuously changes and the sum of numbers of the entire money in the world also changes and both of them do not move together. In other words, the value and the number shown on money are different from each other.

Money is like a gift card that can be exchanged with goods. Gift cards can be exchanged with goods for the same amount of money, but there would be no one who thinks the value of gift cards is equal to the value of money. This is why gift cards are re-sold at cheaper prices than face value. Gift cards have the value of convenience and standard for exchange with the credit of the issuer as security, and money also has the value of convenience and standard for exchange with the credit of the government as security. So, if the government collapses due to a loss of credit, the money used in that system also completely loses its value.

The amount of money existing in the market is continuously increasing due to damage, loss, interests, and credit system in the system of capitalism. Therefore, if it is assumed that the total amount of value existing in the world is a fixed value, the numbers of money corresponding to each value is continuously increasing. This means that the amount of value that can be exchanged with money will decrease. Based on history so far, we know that the total amount of values existing in the world is gradually increasing in a wave form. However increasing the speed of money distributed in the market was faster, so the amount of value that could be exchanged with money gradually decreased. People normally express this as the value of money is decreasing, but it would be more accurate to say that the purchasing power of money is decreasing.

3)   Raw materials

For raw materials, matter normally takes up 100% of the ratio between matter and imagination of the value. It would be easier to understand if we think about them with the element unit. There are many types of elements and you can access them more simply by organizing them according to ancient thoughts rather than dividing one by one. In ancient Western thought, elements were divided into 'water', 'fire', 'air', and 'earth'. In ancient Eastern thought, elements that are the origin of all things were divided into five primary substances which were 'fire', 'earth', 'metal', 'water', and 'wood'. When raw materials are organized based on the above two classification methods, it can be organized as 'water', 'fire', 'air', 'earth', 'metal', and 'wood'. Let's look at 'metal' and 'earth' which are easy to possess as the asset among them.

Gold and silver are representative of the 'metal' asset. Gold and silver have values that make people comfortable and provide pleasures. In particular, they have very excellent intrinsic characteristics as industrial materials. Therefore, metal itself has the value of 100% matter and can be made into materials with greater value through imagination.

Land is representative in the 'earth' asset. The essential value of land is space. Space again provides the value of opportunity. This means there's an opportunity to create new value by filling the space with materials and imagination. Therefore, land itself is an asset that has the value of 100% matter of space and it can exceptionally store additional value with the value of materials and imagination.

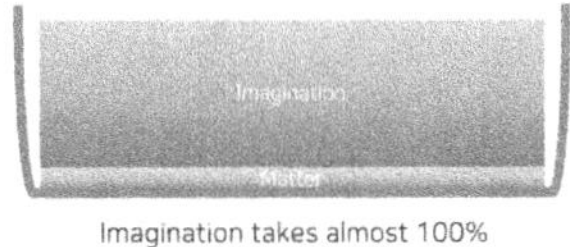
Imagination takes almost 100%

Imagination and matter are combined

Matter takes 100%

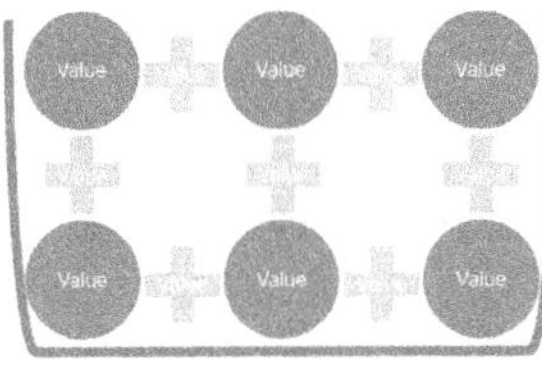
Asset

Positiveness and Gratitude

People are provided with value from the world at every moment of their lives. People get air to breathe, food for energy and pleasure, and clothes to keep warm. Every word from everyone who is taking others is a value and every moment they encounter is also a value. And the value received from the world is stored as a material that can create a new value.

The amount of value accepted would be different depending on one's circumstances and mind. Something of great value to someone may be worthless to others. Love will be worthless for those who have never been impressed by love. And a television program that might be simple fun for some people may help others to make the best business items. Therefore, it is necessary to always accept the value given by the world with a positive attitude.

Positiveness is to accept something as it is. People tend to interpret and judge new values first when they receive them from outside. And they tend not to accept those which they think are not helpful or they don't just like them. This is a negative attitude. Negative attitudes make people reject the values given by the world. Therefore, to grow your own value, you must accept the value given by the world as it is always having a positive mind.

There are some people who only focus on weaknesses or risks. These are typically negative people. No one will share ideas with those who always think negatively and try to find risks when talking about good ideas or businesses. Therefore, it is necessary to always have a positive attitude and a negative attitude should be avoided especially when doing business or making investments.

- Positive attitude: Take some stories or ideas as they are and accept them positively. Then judge them carefully.

- Negative attitude: Listen to stories or ideas while judging and refuse to accept them if they are superficially judged to not be good.

There is nothing you can do on your own without the help of the world. It is possible to work at a company or do business because you have received values such as knowledge and technology from the world. Artists can create works of art because they obtained necessary materials from either nature or people. Athletes can exercise because they obtained the environment and energy appropriate for exercising. No matter how well your imagination can be exercised, if there is no material to add to your imagination, you can't create any additional values. In addition, imagination itself is also a gift from the world. If you accept this fact with a positive attitude, you will naturally have infinite gratitude while living your life. Therefore, positiveness always comes with gratitude and true gratitude leads to the act of reward. If you are truly grateful for the values received from the world, you will repay the world with greater values then the world gives you more value back, making you become more positive. Once a virtuous cycle is structured in this way, your own values will gradually get bigger.

Positiveness and gratitude become interlocked with each other and gradually grow through a virtuous cycle. The more positive you are, the more value you accept, and as a result, the grater gratitude you will have. And the more you feel grateful, the more value you repay to the world and get back again to be more positive. As a result, you become more positive and more grateful.

Luck and Ability

Many people often say "We can't be rich if there is no asset to be inherited," "We can't be rich if we don't have luck," or "Being rich with ability and effort is an old story. It's not feasible anymore nowadays," but you should never think like this. Such thoughts are a kind of negative attitude and they are even foolish. Nothing can be achieved without ability no matter how much luck you have. Luck is an object for use, not magic that makes you succeed automatically.

Luck is an opportunity. If you accept an opportunity, it acts like luck; otherwise it will just pass by. Opportunity is like rain from the sky. Just as it rains when the time comes, opportunity also comes in due time. Even at this moment, it must be raining somewhere and opportunities certainly exist somewhere, too. It is your ability to recognize and catch the opportunities as well as to make good use of them according to your situation. While the opportunities are like rain from the sky, holding more rain means getting more opportunities. To hold more rain, you need to put a container in a rainy place at the time it's raining. To do so, you must know where it rains a lot, have the ability to predict the weather, and have skills to make the container. Let's apply this example to business. Knowing a place where it rains a lot is like knowing the market with a large demand, and predicting the weather is like reading the trends and predicting items that will be in high demand. And the skill of making a container is like the skill of preparing a business that can produce items. And the ability to operate the business well is the ability to make good use of the opportunities you have caught.

When we predict the weather today, we receive the help of the weather forecast. This is same for opportunities. Opportunities are predicted with the help of experts, specific organizations, or people who have information. Therefore, you need a positive attitude to get opportunities. You can get as much luck as possible through various media and people you encounter every moment with a positive attitude.

It would be good to have a bigger container to hold luck. Being big means wide and deep, and width and depth are both important. But in the case of luck, it is better to focus on width rather than depth. This is because the probability of encountering luck increases and the amount of luck that can be held in it at the same time is larger. Therefore, you must widen the container to hold luck by getting materials in all fields including politics, the economy, society, culture and art, and acting in various fields.

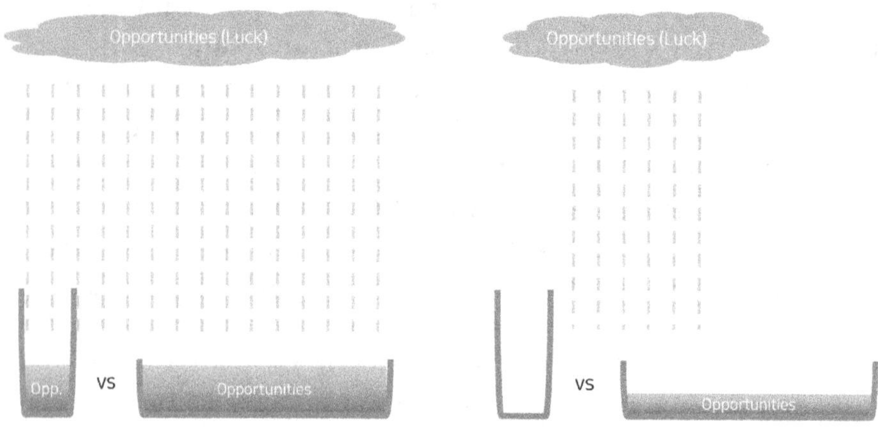

❋ ❋ ❋

The factors I mentioned so far are the ones I think are the most essential in life. In the following parts of this book I will explain further so that it will be easier to understand if you think based on the above explained factors.

PART II. WORK

I worked for money because I couldn't keep a basic life without a salary. Of course, I tried to find the meaning of life through company life with words like reward or self-growth, but no matter how good of a meaning I gave, I couldn't give it more than salary. I was most pleased with a raised salary and was most heated with a frozen salary.

The company said that if I worked sincerely, I could be promoted, take on more important positions, and raise my salary. And some types of people said that playing up to those who are in a higher position is the key to success rather than doing a good job. However nothing touched me that much.

As I worked, I was much more willing to avoid being criticized than trying to contribute to the company. I took great care to not make typos or mistakes, and I acted in order to not look like those who worked loosely.

There was little money left from my salary after food, transportation, and communication expenses, as well as insurance, bills, and other living expenses, but I thought I should be grateful that I had a job that paid me a salary.

Rich Dad Poor Dad says that the rich work for learning, not for money. It might be understood in my head, but I didn't feel great in my heart. After quitting the company that makes electric machines like motors, I decided to focus on learning when I joined another company. And I joined an IT-related company which had nothing to do with my career. It was quite difficult to express accurately about working in a new area, but it seemed I could learn something. I could learn new skills and tendencies, characteristics, and thoughts and the language of people working in different areas.

Just before I finally left the company, I offered to work unpaid for a while. I thought I could get a better feel of the meaning of working for learning if I worked unpaid. Unfortunately, I wasn't able to work unpaid because of a legal restriction, but I worked with the minimum salary that was allowed by law. My relationship with the company was linked by a contract at its face, but the essence was different. I sincerely worked to be helpful to the company and the company thanked me. After eliminating the influence of salary, I could understand the true mission of the company and I could feel the company as a living creature. And I could also feel the meaning of working for learning with my heart.

CHAPTER 1. PLAYERS OF VALUE PRODUCTION

I explained about life generally in part 1, and I will deal with more particular things here in part 2. 'Work' is an indispensable part of our lives. To understand work, you first need to understand the production of values. The reason why the production of values is important is because most values have a large proportion of imagination and are depreciated. That means it should be continuously produced to at least the amount corresponding to the depreciation. In addition, the production of values is a necessary concept in investment which I will further cover later, so please keep it in mind.

Now, economically, the main system that operates the world is the capitalist system. The three requisites for production in the capitalist system are labor, land, and capital. These three factors have organic relations with each other. Labor creates value and land provides the foundation for labor. The capital provides necessary money to make land the foundation of labor and helps to exchange the value created through labor. Each factor has a subject that plays a necessary role.

Laborer

Laborers contribute to the creation of new values by providing their own values of knowledge, skill, and physical energy in the form of labor force. And they get paid in return for the value of their labor.

Produced value must be made in the form of goods or services to be exchanged. In this process, the labor force of the laborer is required.

Laborers act in a way in which they receive salaries by working as office workers, teachers, public officials, lawyers, doctors, etc. or provide goods or services in the form of stores, private institutes, law offices, private hospitals, etc. and receive money.

Landowner

Landowners can also be called businessmen and they contribute to the creation of new value by providing spaces or systems for laborers to exercise labor force. They provide the values of spaces or systems through land, buildings, and business systems that they own and receive money or labor force from laborers in return.

They act in a the form of rental business operators who lend land or buildings to laborers and receive usage fees in return or by providing business systems to exchange new values created by labor force with money.

Capitalist

Capitalists help businessmen and landowners to establish and operate businesses by providing necessary capital or directly supplying money to create new values. Capitalists provide their own capital, which is money, in the form of investments and receive money in return.

They act in the form of national institutes, banks, lenders, and investors.

✳ ✳ ✳

If any one of these three factors is lost in capitalism, the system cannot be maintained. Each factor is part of organic relations that create new values together by exchanging different values with each other. Therefore, it is not easy to say which of these are more important. However, the subject that has the greatest control in the capitalist system is of course capital. This is because it has the most ownership in money which is like blood in the capitalist system. On the other hand, the subject that is treated the best in the capitalist system is land. This is because it plays a role like the heart that provides opportunity for the production of value and actively circulates the blood of the system. This is why businessmen receive far more tax benefits and are treated better than laborers and capitalists.

Activities for producing values do not need to be made through just one factor. For example, if you build a business system and manage it on your own, input the labor force while providing space for labor to laborers, and supply capital to certain investment objects at the same time, it means that you are acting in all factors. If laborers invest in stocks, it means that they are acting in two factors: labor and capital.

Since the type and roles of values provided in each factor are all different, the opportunities for producing and providing values increase when activities of value production are performed in all factors at the same time. Therefore, it is good to perform the activities of value production with balance in all factors of labor, land, and capital. You can see many major companies choose the owner management system and have financial affiliates, and it may be the same reason as mentioned above.

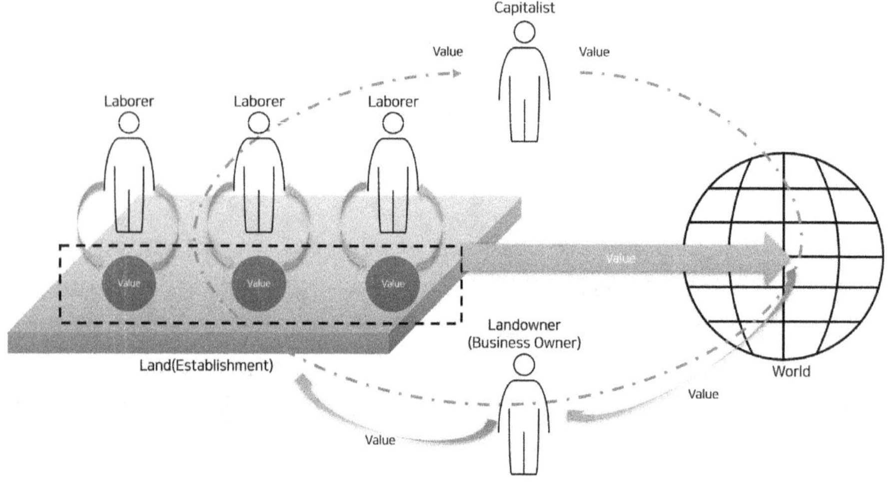

CHAPTER 2.
ABOUT WORK

The nature of work is the exchange of values. In other words, working is to contribute to the increase in value by providing one's own value to the world and being repaid. The value you provide here is imagination or labor force with imagination, and the return is mainly money. Since money is a means of exchange for values, it is necessary to preserve or increase the value of the money by exchanging it with others. I will explain it later in the investment part. Anyway, work must be continued without stopping throughout your life given that it is an exchange of value. It is for both basic survival and a happy life. This is because work provides values to the world and it is an inevitable activity in the process of fulfilling the mission. In this respect, retirement is a turning point that starts other forms of work, generally in the direction of increasing the proportion of imagination and decreasing the proportion of physical labor force in the value provided to the world, not completely stopping work itself.

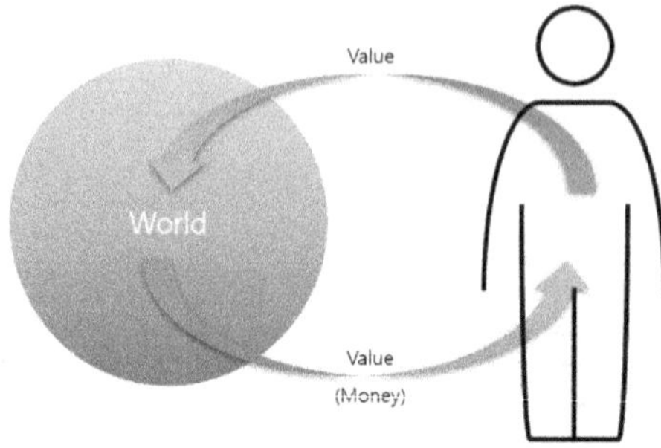

You must have values preserved to provide values. And you need to continuously grow your own values because the value you have is gradually decreasing by depreciation. When you are working, you may think that you are continuously exchanging values, which is working, even if you don't particularly grow your values. However this is not true. The reason you can continuously work is because you are continuously creating values by combining the materials of skills and labor force that you have with imagination. In addition, your skill is developing as you repeat the same work and it itself continuously grows your values. And this is why your salary increases every year as your career accumulates. In general, your life itself is a process of accumulating values. So, your values tend to get bigger and bigger even if you don't consciously make efforts to grow them.

When I explained about the mission, I said that it presents you the direction in which to provide your own value to the world throughout your lifetime. Therefore, there is an area where values can be maximized over a lifetime in the direction suggested by the mission. The mission is to provide the world with the greatest values as it is a lifelong task, and if the values provided to the world are large, it means that the amount of value to be exchanged is large, too. For this reason, you must grow your own values. So, choosing work suitable for the mission is the most efficient way to accumulate great values, and you will fill more of the proportion from your mission given in the form of deficiencies and gain more riches accordingly.

Being capable of doing work means that the values you can provide are large. And being good at work means you can be good at exchanging values. In other words, it means that skill for exchanging values is good. Therefore, you must consider two aspects of growing your own values and developing skills for exchanging.

There will be various ways to grow your values, and I will explain how to grow your values later in this book, but there are no other ways to develop skills for exchanging values than experience and repetition. Therefore, it is better to put more effort into growing values. This is because experience and repetition are accumulated over time and it is difficult to achieve rapid outcomes through effort.

In conclusion, work must be continued throughout a lifetime; it should fit into your mission and effort to grow your values is required. This is how you can increase happiness in your life through work.

CHAPTER 3. WHAT TYPE OF WORK SHOULD YOU DO?

Work is an exchange of value and there are mainly two ways in which to exchange value. The first is to immediately exchange the values you created with other values. The second is to use a kind of leverage, which means to exchange values after growing your own values by adding other values. In other words, these two ways are exchanging values with money immediately and growing values first and then exchanging them with money later, respectively. The first method mainly belongs to the labor factor among the three factors of value production, and the second method belongs to land and capital.

Robert Kiyosaki, the author of *Rich Dad Poor Dad*, explained that the cash flow quadrant is divided into E (Employee), S (Self-Employed), B (Business Owner), and I (Investor). These are the four areas that generate cash, and these areas are related to work, the exchange of values. This is a concept I was inspired by a lot. The 'E' and 'S' divisions belong to the factor of labor and the 'B' and 'I' divisions mainly belong to land and capital among the three factors of production. Robert Kiyosaki placed 'E' and 'S' on the left and 'B' and 'I' on the right. He stated that on average, the rich earn 30% of their income from 'E' and 'S' which are on the left and 70% from 'B' and 'I', which are on the right. If I substitute my theory that we must act in all three factors of value production and put a weight of 33.3% for each factor, 33.3% would be in 'E' and 'S' which are a labor and 66.6% would be in 'B' and 'I' which are land and capital. So, the 3:7 ratio that Robert Kiyosaki stated seems to be reasonable. In this book, the concept of cash flow quadrant just helps explaining the concept, and the criteria used here are the three factors of value production which are labor, land, and capital.

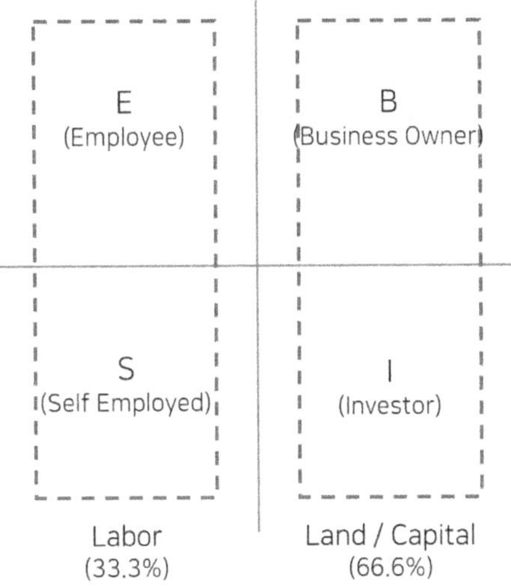

Now, let's look at two ways to work and what direction you must pursue.

Immediate Exchange of Values: Labor – E (Employee), S (Self-employed, professionals)

For occupations that immediately exchange your own values with money, there are office workers, teachers, and public officials who work and receive a salary according to a contract and self-employed people who are paid as much money as they work for on their own without any contract.

For all ages, the preferred form of work for many people seems to be employees. This is probably because people feel it is relatively easy to access and stable. Employees are considered to be stable because a fixed amount of income is guaranteed for a specific period according to a contract. Even if values provided by employees do not meet the expectation of employers, they are paid the same as in the terms of the contract. In particular, occupations like public officials with a guaranteed retirement age and pension are considered as the best in terms of stability.

On the other hand, employees can't receive more than the fixed salary according to their contract, even if values they provide are great. And employees should work for a fixed amount of time according to the labor contract, and the employers, not employees, have control over that time. This means that their freedom is limited. In addition, even if their values are rapidly increased, due to the nature of labor contract, the increase in salary is usually limited.

The self-employed are freer than employers. Their real life might be busier than that of employers, but everything depends on their own free will. For example, they can shorten business time or close their business for a short time depending on their own will even if they make less money. Because there is no fixed labor contract, they have ownership of their time and exercise control over it. For this reason, some people prefer to be self-employed. While employees often provide specific values to their employer and company or occupation and industries, the self-employed can provide values in a wider and more general range. Therefore, the ability to exchange values developed while working is less limited by region, country, time, and so on. In addition, they can receive rewards in proportion to the size of their efforts and values they provide, and they can make more money by making good use of trends or adding other values to their own values.

On the other hand, the self-employed may undergo economic risk if their business doesn't work out well since there is no guaranteed income. That is why people often recognize being self-employed as hard and unstable. And the self-employed have ownership on their time, but each order has an obligation like a contract and limits the freedom of time for short periods. Since the self-employed are similar to the form of business, many people tend to think that it is a business, but it is different. This is because they immediately exchange the values they provide with money.

A professional self-employed person with a professional license and a place of business they own is a form preferred by many people, more so than being stable employees. Generally, this form has similar characteristics and advantages and disadvantages to the general self-employed. Specifically, since it has a high barrier to enter and provides values that are difficult to access, the income is often much higher than that of the general self-employed and employees.

On the other hand, the values provided by the professional self-employed are exchanged at a unit price with a limited range set in the market. And from a large frame, it provides standardized values according to the manual, so it is limited in providing additional values. In other words, they basically make a lot of money, but the opportunities to rapidly make more money are relatively limited.

The biggest characteristic of the immediate exchange of values is that the way to exchange values is just like walking. If moving forward is compared to making money by exchanging values, you can make money only when walking forward. This has both advantages and disadvantages at the same time. The advantage is that anyone can make money if they put in their energy and make an effort. Therefore, this type of work can provide you stability when thinking of money in connection with survival or daily life. However there is the disadvantage that income can disappear as soon as walking stops, and this greatly infringes on the stability. As you get older, you will face the moment of losing energy or having to retire, or a situation where you can't work due to diseases or an injury from an accident. It is just like that that there is always the possibility of an accident even though you don't think that an accident may occur when you walk on the street, and the possibility is very low in reality. Therefore, you must always be ready for the situation where you can't work if you are engaged in work that immediately exchanges values.

If you only work in a way that immediately exchanges values, the possibility to be rich is very slim. The rich want greater freedom while pursuing greater happiness and the amount of time and money required accordingly will also increase. However, the work for immediately exchanging values is far from getting rich because the ownership of time is very limited and increasing the amount of money made is also relatively limited.

You should especially pay more attention to an occupation in which pension is guaranteed. You can easily feel that an occupation with guaranteed pension provides stability, and this may make you to rely too much on the pension itself. And even if there are other good opportunities or you find something you truly want to do, it is not easy to give up a pension and move in other directions. So, you might think that you should maintain that occupation until you retire and you even don't care if there is a better direction. Pension is provided after retirement, so it must always be lower than an earned income. In addition, there is no way to increase income by adding values. As such, if you put too much value on the pension and rely on it and don't pay attention to other ways of exchanging values, there is no possibility to be rich at all.

Exchanging After Growing Values: Land, Capital – B (Business Owner), I (Investor)

Exchanging values after growing them is a method that business owners or investors use. Business owners or investors are not subordinated to a contractual relation that they are obligated to work. Rather, they only do necessary work or something they want to do depending on their will.

While there are some people who try to do business with the expectation that they can make a lot of money, there are some people who think it should never be done due to the fear of a failure of business. In conclusion, there are so many advantages in doing business and it is a must-do type of work that anyone should do without fear if they understand its nature well. In particular, it is essential for a happy life.

To do business, we must have an establishment. This is why business belongs to 'land' among the three factors of value production. An establishment can be a 'machine to earn money' in easy terms. A machine called establishment naturally makes money once energy is supplied. Business owners input values for making establishment and produce new values through the system. And then they exchange them for money.

Conceptually, business owners input the values in making the establishment and the subjects creating the new values within the establishment are laborers hired by the business owners or the system itself. But in reality, most business owners take charge of supplying basic materials to make the establishment add additional values. At this point, supplying basic materials is made in the form of management. You can know one characteristic of the business here. Most business owners are working in the area of land to make the establishment and at the same time, they are working in the area of labor to input the values in the establishment through management.

In the value input to make the establishment, imagination makes up the majority. And the values created by establishment are goods in the form of a product or service after all. The values created here are also occupied by imagination in a large proportion. Values created by imagination have depreciation, so the establishment is just like living things. All living things eventually die if they don't consistently get nutrients. They can be healthy with good nutrients, get weak with harmful nutrients, and die instantly with poison. Therefore, business owners should put good value materials which are good nutrients into their own establishment and they must manage it well to create good values. If the value business owners have is great, the business can operate better.

As I mentioned, there are many advantages in doing business. First, business owners can give their own mission to their establishment since it is created directly by them. Therefore, business itself can be the process of fulfilling the mission in the life of the business owners. Second, there is freedom in business. Since business owners can have complete ownership on the establishment they make, they can also exercise complete control over it. Of course, they can also receive investments or share stakes through joint establishment and they can freely choose to depending on their will and plan. They can also freely choose management methods such as working through direct management or entrusting professional managers which are agents. In addition, there is no fixed period for retirement because there is no contract for work, and the freedom to work as much as they want is guaranteed. Third, basically, business belongs to the factor of 'land' and it prepares the foundation of labor and helps the flow of capital as briefly mentioned earlier. So, business owners can be treated well institutionally and have many benefits including taxes. Fourth, the values created by the business are largely occupied by imagination and the size of the imagination is not limited, so there is an opportunity to make unlimited money depending on what they do. This means that it is very advantageous to live while gaining riches, enjoying freedom, and pursuing happiness. Lastly, it is advantageous for business owners to become investors. Most investors are large organizations such as national institutes or banks, and individuals simply tend to invest in bonds or stocks. However if business owners grow establishments by making successful business, they can be big investors as well as business owners by establishing investment affiliates. In reality, you can see many large companies have investment affiliates.

The reason people have negative views on business is because of the fear of the failure of business. The failure of business can also be said as risk. From an economic point of view, risk means not being able to repay the money borrowed, but the risks of business can be avoided in various ways. One way is to do a business that can be started on a small scale or can provide service goods that require little or no costs to borrow. If you understand the structure that can help manage and avoid risks, you don't need to have fear for the business.

Let's think about the explanation that directly exchanging value is like walking. Exchanging values after growing them through business or investments is like riding a bicycle or driving a car. The biggest characteristic of riding a bicycle or driving a car is inertia. Since exchanging values after growing them has inertia, the income doesn't disappear as soon as the work for putting the values has stopped. Rather, the income gradually decreases until the power of inertia is finally consumed. And we don't even need to step on any pedals or accelerators without resting to make sure the forward momentum doesn't disappear. Business owners or investors can make more than a certain level of income by just putting values at certain intervals. They can even have opportunities to speed them up without making any additional effort by using changes in the external environment such as slope. This is the most decisive characteristic that distinguishes labor from business and investment.

* * *

We looked at the types of work based on the three factors of value production. In short, if we call work for immediately exchanging values as labor and work for exchanging values after growing them as business, business has far more advantages than labor. This doesn't mean that labor is not good. Every type of work comes with learning. Learning is to obtain the materials of value and consequently grow one's own value. There are certainly values that can be obtained only by direct experience. In other words, there are experiences that can be obtained only in a state of being subordinate to labor or contractual relations. Therefore, it is worth it to do labor. However, in the end, you must pursue the ability to act as a business owner after all.

If you start from labor, you have to change in order to do business after doing labor. If you can start business from the beginning, it's also very nice. In both cases, the most important thing is that you must focus on learning and growing your values through everything, such as people you can meet through work, special situations that can be experienced only through work, skills that can be learned, and changes and trends of the industry regardless of the type. And finally, you get to act as a business owner and be happy.

PART III. INVESTMENT

"I earned $300 in a month with my investment on XXX."
"The price of XXX I bought this morning has already increased by 5%."

When my colleagues talked about good stock items while making investments in stocks, my mind was disturbed. I felt that I fell behind because others had made a little bit of money by investing in stocks. When I looked for an item recommended by others, I didn't have the courage to buy because it had already increased a lot. When I bought a stock with urgency, my mind moved with the price which had changed in mere seconds. When it increased by 1%, my heart was happy by 1%; when it decreased by 1%, my heart became anxious by 10%. And I didn't even end up making money in the end.

I was envious of those who bought a house with a mortgage, but I worried about whether those who got a loan and invested in other real estate would eventually go bankrupt. 'Why do they try to invest while getting a loan? It would be better to buy a house with a mortgage and pay off the loan quickly....'

As I studied about real estate investment with interest, I thought 'I should have started it 3 years earlier....' I felt that I had missed a good time and it seemed that it was easier in the past, but difficult now. I thought someone had already taken all the good items and only bad ones remained since people these days are very interested in investment, unlike people in the past. It seemed that the overall real estate price would not increase, but rather decrease because it has already increased a lot at that point.

When I started investing in real estate, my friends worried about me. I still vividly remember one sentence I had heard: "I hope I can meet you for a long time." The meaning was that I'd be in trouble soon by investing. The friend who said this in the past now asks me where and how to invest.

When the total amount of my loans was about 1M USD, my friends worried about me and tried to buy me a drink whenever we met. When the total amount of my loans was about 2M USD, those friends wanted me to buy a drink for them. Of course, with pure and good intentions.

CHAPTER 1. ABOUT INVESTMENT

There are two major axes on economic activities. One is work and the other is investment. Almost everyone works in their lifetime, but they don't often invest. However, investment should be dealt as an essential factor of life just like work. Investment is to appropriately transfer values to assets and eventually to preserve or grow the values contained the in assets. Therefore, not making investments means having values acquired through work only as money a means of exchanging values, and the values can't be preserved and are gradually lost. It is just like forgetting brilliant ideas that come to mind because of not recording them. Just as you need paper to take memo ideas, you need assets to store values. You must pay money to own assets and this is to asset-ize earned money by work. Therefore, work and investment can be considered as connected activities. In other words, the end of work is investment.

Because value is an essential factor in life, you need to understand and accept work and investment which are involved in the activities of creating, exchanging, and storing values as a part of life.

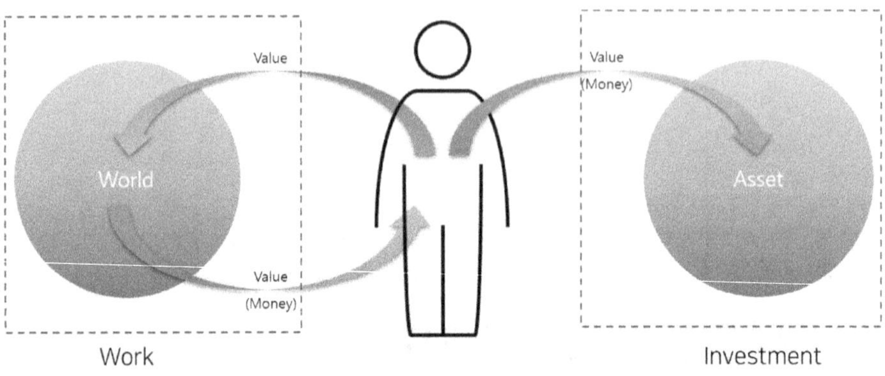

Investment starts with owning assets. Assets include values and the nature of investment is to preserve or grow values. So, fundamental activity for investment is to keep assets with preserved values and to continuously transfer assets with changing values into other assets at appropriate times. In this context, investment would be very easy if we could judge whether the value contained in the assets is variable or not and if the values will increase or decrease. Unfortunately, it is not easy to judge the variability and direction of value changes and the situations we encounter in reality are very complicated.

Judging the variability and direction of value changes is made based on the ratio of matter and imagination. Assets such as gold and silver, for example, contain values with the proportion of 100% matter, so there is no variability on the values. This means that you can invest in gold and silver as assets that preserve their values. Assets with a high proportion of imagination such as stocks, however, can be invested in as an asset that grows its value with its high variability on values. In this case, the entire value grows when the input of imagination is more than the depreciation of values, and they decrease vice versa. To make such good investments, the ability to judge variability and the direction of value changes contained in assets is required.

It is not easy to judge only with variability and the direction of value changes, and the fact that you should buy ownership of assets with money makes investment much more complicated and difficult. The amount of currency continuously increases over time. The increase in the amount of currency degrades the ability to exchange the value of money and it eventually leads to the increase of the price of the assets. A bigger problem is that not all asset values increase at the same proportion as the amount of currency increases.

Let's compare this to seawater. The height of the sea level varies in all places due to the tides such as high tide and low tide. So, when assuming that the amount of seawater is continuously increasing, the height of the sea level will not increase at a constant proportion in all places, but will vary depending on changes in the tide. You can easily understand this if you think of the increase in the amount of currency as the increase of seawater, various types of assets as various places on earth, and the degree for reflecting prices of assets as the high and low tides. While tides in nature have regular cycles and patterns with tide-generating forces, the reflection on assets appears depending on people's attention and its cycle and pattern are not constant. As such, the facts that a kind of tidal change appears in the price of assets depending on people's attention and the amount of currency steadily increases are the factors that make investment the most difficult.

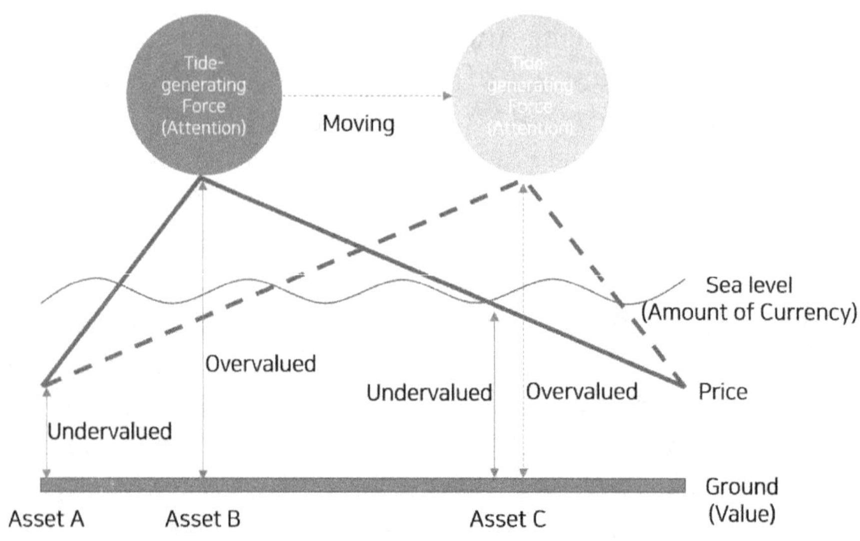

In summary, you need to have the ability to judge variability and the direction of asset value changes and tidal changes in asset prices to make good investments. When certain asset values are in the direction of increasing and prices are relatively headed in the direction of decreasing, these assets are more undervalued. The opposite is to be overvalued. Purchasing undervalued assets, selling overvalued assets, and purchasing undervalued assets again is what making good investments is all about. Theoretically, you can think of a number of patterns. In reality, purchasing 'asset G' and selling 'asset H' among the following patterns is the most desirable in investment activities.

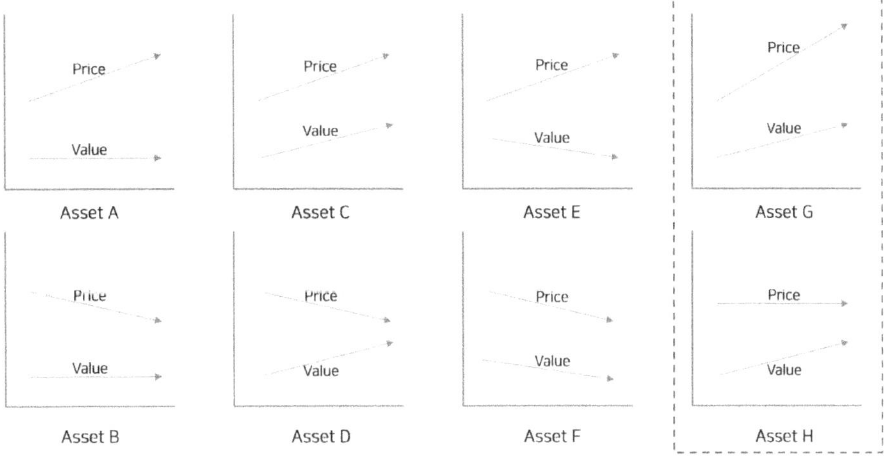

To have the ability to make good investments, you need to study a lot and have practical experiences. Specifically, you need to analyze and judge wide and various ranges of areas such as politics, society, economy, technology, culture, and art and be able to read changes in people's attention. However, it takes too much time and effort to accumulate knowledge and experience in all areas. In addition, you must have set standards to measure the size of values, but the numbers on money are the only standards you can use. And since the size of values you can exchange with the numbers shown on money is constantly changing, you must track and utilize the number information exchanged at various times over a long period of time. Therefore, it is efficient to entrust specific analysis to experts and to develop the intuition to make comprehensive and macroscopic judgment by gathering as much as information as possible.

In conclusion, developing intuition on values and prices is a way to make good investments by constantly studying all areas and experiencing actual investment a lot by collecting and judging the specific analysis of experts.

CHAPTER 2. ASSET CLASSES

Making investments is to own assets, so you must understand assets in order to invest. As mentioned before, there are many forms and types of assets. I classify assets according to their characteristics in order to make a portfolio related to assets and call them 'asset classes'. Asset classes classified according to this include 'self-asset', 'currency asset', 'basic asset', 'cash flow asset', 'value growth asset', and 'value defense asset'. Now, let's look at the characteristics of each asset class.

Self-Asset (Oneself)

Self-asset is the most important asset people can own because it is the subject of all activities including economic activities. In addition, it is an asset that can contain infinite value and grow infinitely, having the highest economic value.

Unlike other assets that you should pay money to obtain ownership, self-asset is the one that starts with full ownership from the beginning. The universe provides an environment where people can cooperate and grow each other's values, but it can be used to just increase other's values if you don't grow values on your own. This can be said to mean being under the control of the world. If you don't exercise your subjecthood and just leave yourself under the control of the world, your ownership will be easily infringed upon and taken by others. Therefore, it is necessary to keep and manage your own ownership.

As you live your life, there may be countless situations in which you should make a contract with yourself as collateral. Contractual relations are made in various forms such as labor contracts and credit loan contracts, and they are not all easy to avoid. Therefore, even if you make a contract with yourself as collateral, you must live with the mindset and goal of terminating the contract and regaining your full ownership as soon as possible.

We often use the expression to invest in ourselves. Since investment is to transfer the values we have into assets in an appropriate manner, investing in ourselves means to accept and store the values from the world well. You can grow your values by materializing values from the world and adding your own imagination. The world tends to control people, but it firstly tries to provide people as many values as possible. So, normally you can grow your values by just accepting those values well. However, if you make investments in yourself more actively and systematically through reading, learning, training, and exercising, you can grow your values more efficiently and rapidly.

It is not easy to measure the size of values and it is even more difficult to measure the value of a person, not goods. However it is somehow possible to make a standard and rough estimate by using investments you can get through the business plan you make, your salary, and the limit of credit loan presented by your labor contract and the coverage limit you can receive by a signed insurance contract, etc. Through these methods, you need to regularly measure and judge the value changes of your own self-asset.

Currency Asset (Money)

Currency has the value of the ability for exchanging based on the credit value of institutions and systems. This kind of ability for exchanging is represented by numbers. Since the purchasing power included in the numbers continues to decrease, it is not proper to refer to currency as an asset in terms of investment. However, since most of the value exchange is made through currency, you need to place currency in one asset class to manage it. But again, you must not think that the values are well maintained while holding money for a long period of time, more than necessary.

Currency plays a role in helping to replace values in each asset through the ability for exchanging when making investments. And it makes it possible to operate the asset when it is necessary. As you do economic activities, you may sometimes face the crisis of liquidity. This refers to the time when the currency required for operating assets is insufficient.

In conclusion, you must be careful not to make the mistake of treating currency as an asset for preserving or growing values. At the same time, you must be aware of your appropriate amount of currency asset necessary to make investments or operate assets.

Basic Asset (Accommodation)

The most essential and basic factors for maintaining a basic life are food, clothing, and shelter. Among these, clothing and food are subject for just exchanging, not investing, since they are continuously consumed. But shelter is different because it has the value of matter that is not consumed as space. Shelter provides the foundation and space for people to live as well as physical protection and spiritual peace. In other words, shelter is an asset that constantly provides value and contains the values people own. That is why I refer to it as a basic asset.

Shelters are often borrowed in the form of rentals rather than direct ownership. However, borrowing means you can't have complete ownership and therefore can't exercise control. If you don't own a shelter, you can't put in your own values. Shelter is where you spend most of the time in your life and is a place that provides values to you for the longest period of time. Therefore, it is an efficient subject for investment since the more you put your values into shelter, the more values you can receive over time. So, it is a great loss in your life to borrow your shelter, not owning it, which means not having the basic asset.

Shelter, which is a basic asset, is the one you must acquire first after starting economic activities and you must own better assets depending on the size of the values you've accumulated. In other words, you should change your shelter into a better one as your assets increase. This is because better basic assets can contain more values. And it is also because if you have more values, you can constantly receive values such as the greater convenience of life and inspiration. Therefore, it is very important to own a good basic asset and by this your life can be enriched in various ways.

Cash Flow Asset (Profitable Asset)

The cash flow asset is an asset that regularly provides returns by working on its own while storing values itself. The asset itself becomes an automated operating system. There are various types of cash flow assets including buildings for rent, dividend stocks, bonds, and establishments. It is an asset that makes it possible to make investments in the concept of growing values since it can not only store values but also create and exchange values on its own.

There are many advantages in storing values as a cash flow asset. First, cash created by the asset is helpful in practical life. It creates an environment where you can focus on learning, not money while working, and provides a foundation to have ownership on your own time. I was also able to quit my job easily when cash created from the cash flow asset became double my salary. In addition, the cash flow asset creates acceleration in growing values and gaining riches through investment. This is because the newly created cash flow is accumulated in investments equally. And once cash flow is created, it eliminates the burden of repaying loan interests, making good use of leverage and increasing the effect of investments.

Making regular cash created through the cash flow asset more than living expenses is the most practical condition for making a life structure that pursues happiness, gains freedom, and makes riches follow you.

Value Growth Asset (Margin Asset)

The value growth asset is an asset that absorbs external values and grows its values when the values are contained. There are various types including real estate (especially land), stocks, works of art, and establishments, and it is an asset that enables investment in the concept that grows values just like the cash flow asset.

It is not easy to distinguish the value growth asset as completely different type from cash flow asset. This is because cash flow can be created through the value growth asset and the cash flow asset itself can absorb external values to grow its values. We can often express them as a profitable asset and margin asset, respectively, and they must be clearly distinguished according to the proportion of profits and margins and the purpose of investment. In other words, if the purpose is to create cash flow, you must invest in a cash flow asset with a high proportion of profit. If the purpose is to do other investments or activities by using values grown after a certain period of time, you must invest in a value growth asset with a high proportion of margin. Profitable and margin assets can be distinguished based on the expected rate of return. In my experience, the average annual rate of return for the profitable asset would be from 5% to more than 20% and the margin asset would be from 30% to more than 50%. For example, when you invest $10,000, you can expect a return of about $40-160 per month for a profitable asset and more than $10,000 after three years for a margin asset.

By making the investment, you preserve and grow the values you have and can increase entire assets. In terms of the activities of investment alone, it is the value growth asset that plays the biggest role in increasing the entire amount of assets. Therefore, you must actively utilize the value growth asset when making investments.

Value Defense Asset (Gold, Silver)

Most values existing in the world include the imagination and values created by this imagination always depreciate. Therefore, it is necessary to constantly check whether imagination is being added to each asset when storing your own values in the asset. At the same time, you must prepare for the situation in which the depreciation of the values is proceeding faster than the input of imagination. At this point, an asset that can play a big role is a value defense asset.

The value defense asset is an asset that only has values of matter, not imagination. In other words, it is an asset with no loss or growth of values. Gold and silver are the representative ones in this asset. Since other types are not commonly accessible, it is better to start with gold and silver only. Except for some cases in which you were completely wrong or made errors of judgement in investments, the cases in which an asset rapidly loses its values mainly occur at the time when there is an external crisis in the large flow such as a financial crisis. During this time, people's psychology becomes unstable and currencies are concentrated in the safe assets. And the values of gold and silver remain the same, but the price increases with the concentrated currencies. Therefore, gold and silver are overvalued, and if you can use them to recover or restructure your portfolio appropriately, you can defend values in such crises situations.

When dealing with value defense assets, it is not right to think "I earn money with the increased price of gold". Value defense assets are only for defending. If you fully understand and follow the composition of the portfolio and risk management which I will explain further, you will find that the situations where you should sell your value defense assets occur extremely rarely, such as a meltdown of the financial system due to cataclysm including war, sovereign default, and natural disasters.

✽ ✽ ✽

I classified the assets into classes so far. To avoid risk and instability in investment, you must understand each asset class and create standards. Making investments in self-assets is the most basic and important, so you need to make it a daily habit. And for the rest of the asset classes, it is necessary to make investments in a planned and strategic order and portion.

CHAPTER 3. PORTFOLIO COMPOSITION

I explained about the concepts necessary for investing so far. Let's look at the direction and method of investment from now on. Portfolio composition is to set a proportion for each asset class based on the size of values contained in the assets. The reason for composing the portfolio is to guarantee basic living with cash flow while increasing the size of the entire assets and to make effective investments that can defend the crisis that may occur at any time. Therefore, portfolio composition is an essential factor to gain and keep riches, and it exercises very strong power in your life from an economic point of view. Making a portfolio with an appropriate proportion within the shortest time is the first key factor to make good investments.

Again, it is very difficult to measure the values contained in the assets, and the numbers on currency for which each asset is exchanged, which is a price, is not fixed. For this reason, all the numbers to be explained will be based on the current price, and you need to regularly judge changes of the asset prices and changes in the values accumulating the data.

You must understand leverage, too. Leverage simply means

to get a loan. Leverage is required when making an investment because it maximizes the effectiveness of the investment, but interest always follows with a loan. Therefore, you must know the amount of interest exactly when using leverage and of course, the amount should be within the range you can bear. Keep in mind that the fact that you should use leverage as much as possible means that it should be made within the range in which you can afford to pay interest. And I would like to mention here that the proportion of portfolio composition must be based on the amount invested by you except for leverage. That is, it should be based on the amount of net asset prices.

When making investments, the appropriate proportion of investment for each asset class is as follows.

- Basic asset: 30%

- Cash flow asset: 35%

- Value growth asset: 25%

- Value defense asset: 10%

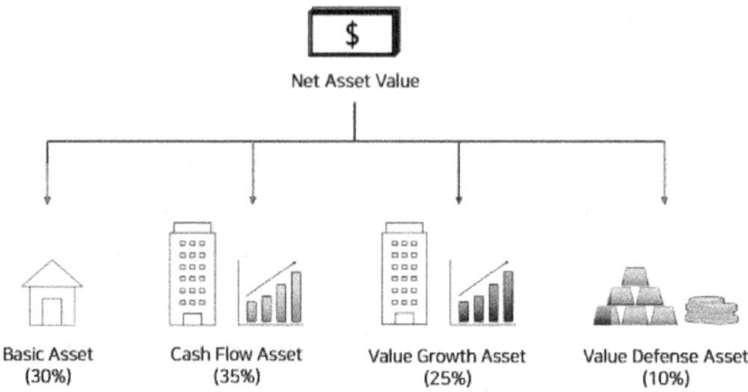

An investment on self-asset here is excluded because it can't be expressed in numbers and it is an activity that must be maintained through living habits. And the currency asset is also excluded because it is not the subject for the investment and it basically doesn't fit the concept and purpose of investment. I will explain about the proper amount of currency assets later in the chapter on risk management.

Basic Asset

Basic asset is the first one to acquire when making a portfolio. This is because it is quite literally a basic asset. In addition, once you acquire basic asset which stays for the longest amount of time in your life, the values you can get from it increase. So, it would be very efficient.

If there is no basic asset, you can't exercise complete control on one axis among the factors of food, clothing, and shelter which are essential for living, and that means you just let the world control and wield you. Therefore, you must have basic assets as soon as possible. However, it is not easy to own a house, which is a basic asset. In general, houses are very expensive, so it is rare to acquire them right away after you start economic activity. This is why most people rent a house and it makes it harder for them to save money. People even give up purchasing houses. Therefore, exact goals and plans are required. Let's take an example with an office worker who has no assets and no loans, but just started economic activity. If they save more than 30% of their average monthly income for 3 to 5 years and use maximum leverage, they can buy a house at around 60-80 times the value of their average monthly income. The maximum leverage here is the leverage that has mobilized all credit loans, not just mortgage loans. For example, a person who earns $2,000 per month on average can save more than $600 per month and buy a house that costs about $140,000 in four years. This can be sufficiently possible if you make a simulation by using spreadsheets, and you can see that the interest is also affordable.

As such, if you imagine that you can buy a house that is 70 times the average of your income, it might not look so attractive because you may think that a house with that price is not very good. However, you must know that it is almost impossible to buy a good house that everyone would prefer with ordinary savings. Acquiring such a good house at once may be a lifelong task or most likely it may be impossible.

But let's think of it in other ways. To buy a house that is 70 times more than your income, you should be patient and save money for 3 to 5 years. This time may be hard and painful, but in the meantime, it would be a time in which to study and prepare a strategy for your asset portfolio. If you can get the same return as the value growth asset from the basic asset through such study and preparation, you can expect more than 30% returns per year through basic assets. In the end, the time required to compose an entire asset portfolio will be faster through a house you own. Indeed, it's possible.

Once you own a house, a lot of changes are made internally. You can feel psychological stability and the sense for feeling economic flow will develop. Just one experience gained after studying, executing, and seeing the results of the judgements made by you can be a turning point in your life. So, there is no need to be disappointed that a house that can be purchased with the money saved for 3 to 5 years looks rather poor. Once you start making investments, you can get explosive inertia. For me, it took a long time to buy my first house, but it just took 2 years to compose my entire portfolio after that. This is because I acquired a good basic asset first.

Speed is important to own basic assets. If you think it is not good time to buy a house under the current economic flows, you wait a little bit more or invest in other assets first, then the time taken to own basic assets and build your entire asset portfolio will be gradually longer. There are always some assets undervalued regardless of the economic flows in any form of assets. Acquiring undervalued basic assets as quickly as possible is the fastest way to build the entire asset portfolio and increase asset value in terms of investment.

Cash Flow Asset

The cash flow asset can be said to be the flower of investment.

This is my favorite asset type because if the asset makes cash regularly, real life becomes enriched, returns that can be earned through investment can be relatively accurately calculated, and it is also fun to use leverage actively. And after all, it is a cash flow asset that allows you to completely regain ownership of your own time.

It is good to start with real estate when making investments in the cash flow asset. Real estate can become collateral that has a certain substance and is easy to evaluate, so it is easy to make a loan through this. Therefore, it is easy to use leverage, the risk is relatively low, and calculation for the return is easy, making you compose portfolio systematically. Since the real estate asset has low variability, there is a limit to the rate of return. But the stability is also equally high, so it is desirable to make cash flow from real estate assets more than average living expenses and then invest in other assets with high variability and returns.

When utilizing leverage, it is good to use it based on more than a 2% difference between the loan interest rate and expected return rate without leverage. For example, if you can receive a loan with an interest rate of 3% per year with the collateral of any cash flow asset, the expected return rate without leverage should be more than 5% per year. At this point, a larger difference between the loan interest rate and the expected return rate without leverage is better. This is because it can be safe even if the actual rate of return falls or the interest rate of the loan increases due to various variables. And the actual rate of return will be better when the amount of the loan is larger. Let's look at the calculation below. Please note that this is a simple calculation that doesn't consider any various additional costs.

Sale Price	$ 900,000		
Interest on Loan	3%		
Expected Rate of Return	5%		
Expected Monthly Income	$ 3,750		
Ratio of Loan	40%	60%	80%
Loan Amount	$ 360,000	$ 540,000	$ 720,000
Monthly Interest	$ 900	$ 1,350	$ 1,800
Investment	$ 540,000	$ 360,000	$ 180,000
Monthly Income after Paying Interest	$ 2,850	$ 2,400	$ 1,950
Rate of Return	6.3%	8.0%	13.0%

You can expect a return from 8% to more than 15% by actively using leverage the in case of general real estate cash flow assets. As you continue to make investments in cash flow assets, you will naturally come to know about various types of assets. There are many cases with high risk as well as a higher rate of return than real estate. If you make cash flow equal to your monthly average expenses though real estate first and then make cash flow with a similar amount in various forms of assets, it can be considered that you primarily completed making investments in the cash flow asset class from the composition of your portfolio. Here, it is good to keep the cash flow created through real estate assets at at least 50% of the total of the cash flow asset class in terms of stability.

Value Growth Asset

When composing your portfolio, you first need to own basic assets. You need to choose between cash the flow asset and value growth asset depending on your situation and tendency. If you are not young and do not have that long of a time to earn money, it would be better to choose cash flow, but if you are young and just started earning money, it would be better to choose the value growth asset first. This is because the value growth asset has a higher expected rate of return, making the composition of your portfolio faster. And it would be more efficient since you can focus more on growing values of your own in the time left by just checking the margin rather having a management point to concern whenever cash flow regularly occurs.

When making investments in value growth assets, it is good to start with real estate, especially with land. The reason is similar to that of cash flow assets, and it is also better in terms of stability for value growth assets. This is because it would be very rare to have a loss of more than 30% with real estate unless you are being swindled or made an extremely bad judgment. It is necessary to make your portfolio safely while carefully learning even if it takes some time before you can completely build your portfolio.

It is not easy to use leverage for value growth assets unlike cash flow assets. This is because it is quite difficult to cover the loan interest in a situation where additional cash flow is not made. In particular, interest that is periodically generated would feel like a loss and makes you psychologically impatient, giving you poor judgment. Even if there is little leverage used for value growth assets, when it goes well, you can expect about a return of 40% per year. This way, you can increase the entire amount of your portfolio's assets by around 10% per year with only value growth assets.

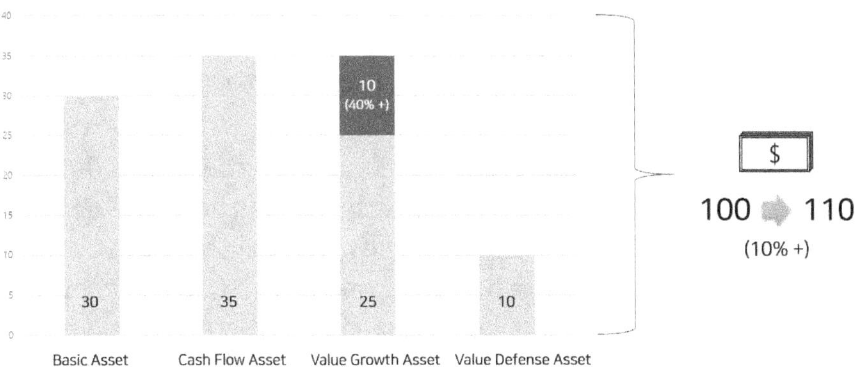

Value Defense Asset

The value defense asset is marked with a side dot in the composition of the portfolio. It adds solidity to the portfolio and provides you the power to defend against any crisis. Gold and silver are assets that perfectly preserve their own values and are easily accessible and commonly used everywhere. So, you must own gold and silver as a value defense asset.

One thing to keep in mind is that you must own them in a physical form. You can make investments in various forms such as ETF, funds, and passbooks, but the essence of the value defense asset is literally a defense for crises. I mentioned that you don't sell value defense assets unless there is an extreme situation such as war or sovereign default. This is because a form other than the real form is meaningless in those situations.

In the case of value defense assets, there is no change in value and you can only judge people's attention level, so it is easier to judge than other assets. However, there are complicated things to consider such as the fact that the price of gold and silver do not move together, the price of silver is more variable than that of gold, and you must consider safe storage in order to own real gold and silver. Therefore, you need to study it separately and set your own standard. For example, you can judge what is more advantageous to own at the current time by setting the gold-silver ratio and using indicators in an appropriate manner. To build such a standard, it would be enough to read just 2 or 3 books related to gold and silver.

Lastly, the most important principle for the value defense asset is that you must own the real thing. All the value defense assets owned by "fake" means, and not the real thing are useless. This means that you must buy gold and silver with an accurate weight and purity. If you keep just this type of thing, the investment in value defense assets is 99.99% successful. It doesn't matter if you buy gold and silver at a relatively expensive price. This is because the price variability according to the general economic flow is nothing compared to the situation where gold and silver should be used for the purpose of defense.

CHAPTER 4. RISK MANAGEMENT

Once the portfolio is composed and each asset is acquired in proportion to each class, the next thing to do is risk management. The nature of risk in economic activities is the inability to pay back the money borrowed from others. In other words, the risk always starts with a loan. When you get a loan, interests are incurred that must be paid back at a regular period. If you repay the principal and interest well according to the contract terms, there will be no problem at all. However, if you can't pay back the principal and interest due to various variables and circumstances, there is the risk such as the possibility of losing ownership of the assets you own.

To build your portfolio in the shortest period of time you must utilize leverage according to the asset class. Therefore, building a portfolio comes with a certain amount of risk, and managing this risk is the second key factor for making a good investment.

Then, let's look at loans, a source of risk. The most important thing for a loan is collateral. Loans always come with collateral. From the lender's side, they set the collateral in case the lent money can't be collected. If the money lent is not collected, they take ownership of the collateral and recover the principal and interest by selling it. If the price left after disposing of the collateral is less than the principal and interest, a more serious problem occurs. But from the standpoint of lenders, they take special care about this part, so this won't happen often. In the case of a credit loan, you may feel that there is no collateral, but the collateral of a credit loan is credit itself. Credit is a value created by the relationships and achievements accumulated in one's life. Therefore, if you can't pay back the money after getting a credit loan, you will decrease the value of your credit among the values contained in your self-asset. All loans have collateral and if you fail to pay back the principal and interest on the loan, you will lose the ownership of the collateral. So, it is very important to know what you set as collateral for the loan.

You must not set the collateral as anything other than the target asset, which is an object for investment when using leverage. For example, if you get a loan to own the asset called A, the collateral has to be limited to asset A only. It means you must avoid taking asset B or C that you already own as collateral to have asset A. This ensures that other assets are not affected and the management of risk itself is easier even in the worst situation where you can't overcome the risk. The only exception is to utilize a credit loan together with the original loan. In particular, you might have no choice other than to use a credit loan when initially acquiring a basic asset. And sometimes you need to use a credit loan when acquiring a cash flow asset. In this case, you should use a credit loan in a situation where you can pay it back within 6 months except for the case of an acquisition of an initial basic asset. This is because all of the initial settings such as leases and paybacks are completed within 6 months after making the investment. For example, if there is asset that has a price of $100,000 and you can set the rent deposit at $5,000, there is no problem in using a credit loan for the $5,000 rental deposit that can be received after acquiring the asset.

Unlike the portfolio composition which is based on the proportion of each asset class to the total net asset prices, risk management is based on the proportion of the amount of the loan principal for each asset compared to the price that can be exchanged at present time. In short, it is based on the loan principal compared to the current price of the asset. Appropriate loan limits for each asset class are as follows. Loan limit here means the loan for each asset unit, not the total average of all the assets included in each asset class.

Self-Asset: 5%

Self-asset is an asset completely owned by oneself from the beginning. Therefore, there is no loan you have from the start. However, if you use your own self-asset as leverage, for example, when having basic assets, a credit loan may occur. The credit loan made at this time must be repaid the fastest among all loans. You must regularly check the loan limits you can receive, and you should make a credit loan at less than 5% of the limit once a credit loan occurs. For example, if the limit of a credit loan you can receive is $100,000 and you get a loan for $50,000 to acquire a basic asset, you should make the amount of the loan under $5,000 by starting to repay the loan immediately. In fact, it is almost the same as making a credit loan be 0%. The reason for setting it at 5% is because you will have the ability to repay the amount at any time if your portfolio is well composed.

Basic Asset: 20%

You must make the best use of leverage when owning the basic asset at first. Once you own the asset, you should lessen the loans received with the collateral of the basic asset itself as less than 20% of the asset price. For example, if your house can be traded at $100,000 currently, you should make the loan principal less than $20,000. There must be no loss of ownership due to risk especially in the case of basic assets. Considering the proportion of the portfolio, 20% of the price of basic risk is about 6% of the total net asset amount, meaning you may bear such risk. And usually you can secure about 6 months of funds for risk management if there is any problem related to the house, such as the occurrence of a lease contract problem. In this case, if the ratio of the loan is less than 20%, it would be easy to set the plan for the asset and exercise control within given time.

Cash Flow Asset: 75%

The cash flow asset is an asset with which leverage should be actively utilized because the more leverage is used, the higher return can be gained. Therefore, it is an asset owned by getting as many loans as possible. And once it is owned, the loan should be made at 75% of the asset price. In this case, if the asset is a real estate asset, you can receive a rental deposit in most cases. This rental deposit is a mortgage loan with a 0% interest rate. Therefore, the loan at 75% also includes the rental deposit. For example, if you have an asset cost of $100,000, you should make the sum of the general mortgage loan and rental deposit at $75,000.

In the case of risk management for other asset classes, it is good to set the loan ratio small, such as less than 5% or 20%. On the other hand, it is good to keep it at 75% in case of the cash flow asset class. This is because cash flow assets are relatively unlikely to have a crisis situation and they can increase the efficiency by using leverage. So, they can manage risk at an appropriate level and obtain a high return at the same time.

Value Growth Asset: 20%

It is better to not utilize leverage when owning a value growth asset. You must always accurately judge the values and price changes over time and catch the right time to exchange, but your judgment can be blurred by impatience when the interest occurs regularly. In addition, for the value growth asset you have no choice but to make predictions based only on intuition, unlike the cash flow asset with which you can accurately calculate the rate of return to some degree. Therefore, this asset is more vulnerable to inaccurate predictions or unexpected variables. In conclusion, it's better not to use leverage for the value growth asset, but in case you use it, you must make loans for less than 20% of the asset price. This is corresponding to about 5% of the net asset price amount, and there will be no big difficulty to manage the risk.

Value Defense Asset: 0%

The reason you make the value defense asset as the portfolio is to preserve the value you own with the asset and defend the risk at a catastrophic level. Therefore, it is not fundamentally right to utilize leverage that inevitably comes with risk while acquiring value defense assets. This is why the loan limit of the value defense asset is 0%.

* * *

Currency asset must be specifically covered in the risk management. This is because it can be the primary means for all risk management and most of the risk should be covered only by currency asset. Currency asset are set by holdings, not the concept of loan limit.

Currency Asset: About 3-6 times the average monthly expense

Everyone has an amount of cash regularly required such as basic living expenses, loan interests, and other expenditures. You just need to calculate all of these expenditures and keep it at about 3-6 times the amount of your monthly expenses required on average. For example, if your average monthly expenditure is $1,000, you can keep it between $3,000 and $6,000. This is used as a primary means to defend against risk. In other words, it is the cash required to solve a crisis of large flow that comes from the change in unexpected external environment such as a financial crisis or epidemic, a temporary crisis of liquidity in the cash flow asset, or an individual crisis such as accidents or diseases. Except for the situations in which people can't prepare with their own power such as being involved in serious crimes or having rare incurable diseases, most of the crisis situations come in proportion to the size of one's own assets. At this time, if you have about 3-6 times your average monthly expense in cash, you can solve most of them or at least have time to solve them. In my experience, if the portfolio is well composed, the crisis can be regulated within 3 months in general and can be resolved within 6 months at most. If the amount of surplus (income - expense) accumulated every month is more than the average monthly expense, it would be enough to have cash corresponding to 3 months. Otherwise, you can keep cash corresponding to 6 months, and then you can defend against almost all risks.

The type of currency asset you have must be the currency that is commonly used in the society you belong to. However, if you plan to hold it for about 6 months, it is also good to have 50% of it in the basic currency and the remaining 50% in another currency. When having other types of currency, you must use the major currencies such as the Euro, British Pound, or Japanese Yen.

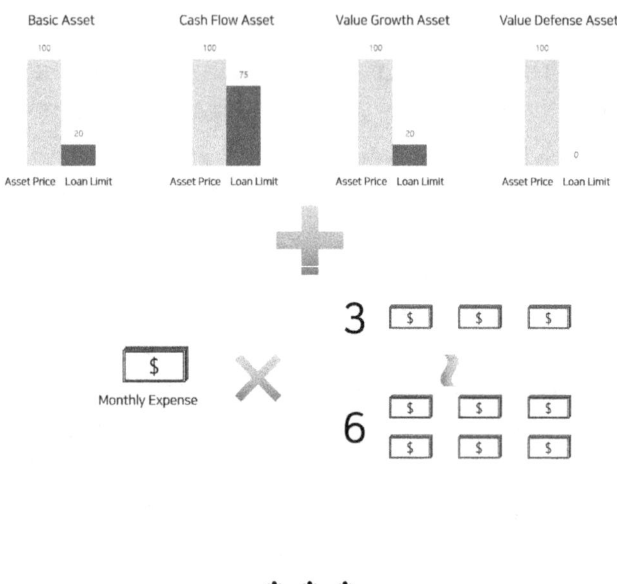

* * *

The way to manage risk is to clean up and recover from a loan. If there is no loan, of course there is no risk. However, to use a powerful tool of leverage that can't be ignored in the investment, it is necessary to manage risk rather than eliminating it. If you compose your portfolio as I mentioned above and keep the ratio of the loan as above, risk can be easily managed.

The order is also important in cleaning up the loans to manage risk. The order of cleaning up the loans is to pay back the credit loan first and then repay the mortgage loan on the asset. Even if the interest rate on the credit loan is the lowest, you must clean up the credit loan first. This is because credit is the most important collateral among all types of collateral. In addition, setting the collateral means that there is a possibility to lose the ownership on the target asset. You should avoid the possibility of lost ownership due to the mortgage for your credit. If this happens, it is a very serious and also very unpleasant thing. Once cleaning up the credit loan, you should clean up the loans in the order of assets that significantly exceed the appropriate loan ratio mentioned above. Among them, the loans with high interest rates should be cleaned up in order. For example, you can judge the order for cleaning up the loan as follows.

Type of Asset	(a) Limit / Price	(b) Loan (+Deposit)	(c) Ratio of Loan	(d) Interest Rate	(e) Appropriate Rate	(f) Excessive Ratio	Order for Repayment
Self-asset (Credit loan)	$ 100,000	$ 1,000	10%	2.5%	5%	200%	1 (Credit loan)
Basic asset (Accommodation)	$ 500,000	$ 200,000	40%	3.0%	20%	200%	3 (Order of excessive ratio)
Cash flow asset 1	$ 500,000	$ 450,000	90%	6.0%	75%	120%	5 (Same excessive ratio => Order of interest rate)
Cash flow asset 2	$ 300,000	$ 270,000	90%	5.0%	75%	120%	6 (Same excessive ratio => Order of interest rate)
Value growth asset 1	$ 400,000	$ 120,000	30%	4.0%	20%	150%	4 (Order of excessive ratio)
Value growth asset 2	$ 200,000	$ 100,000	50%	2.0%	20%	250%	2 (Order of excessive ratio)
$(c) = (b) / (a)$ $(f) = (e) / (c)$							

Once you've built up your asset portfolio, the level of risk becomes very high and the proportion of asset classes in the portfolio would be very different from the beginning after managing the risk. And if the portfolio is rebuilt according to the appropriate ratio, the risk level increases again. Doing risk management after building the portfolio is one cycle of the investment, and as this cycle is repeated, the size of the entire asset gradually increases. And of course, the ability to compose the portfolio and manage risk improves and the efficiency increases as the investment cycle is repeated.

CHAPTER 5. THE FOUR SEASONS OF INVESTMENT

After having one cycle of investment from the composition of a complete portfolio to risk management, investing becomes a game you can enjoy. You should do an investment like a game that you can enjoy, not a gamble in which you can lose everything when you bet wrong. To do so, you need to finish one complete investment cycle as quickly as possible. In other words, one complete investment cycle is a kind of license to participate in the investment game. If you are good at the game, the size of the entire asset rapidly increases and if you are not good at game, the size of the asset slowly increases.

To play a game well, you must understand how to play and have your own standard for judgment. The way to play a game well is simple, it is to sell the overvalued assets you own and purchase good undervalued assets. The standard for judging overvalued and undervalued assets is the changes in values and money flows according to the people's attention. Based on these standards, you can sell the overvalued assets you own and buy undervalued assets.

You should understand the cycle in which people's psychology changes and judge the timing well to smoothly perform your strategy in the investment game. As there are four seasons in nature, there are also four seasons in economic flow. The people's minds move and good investment targets change according to the four seasons appearing in the economic flows. I call this cycle in economic flow "the four seasons of investment". While the four seasons of nature change at a constant cycle with the revolution of the earth, the four seasons of investment change according to the economic cycle. Economic cycles appear irregularly such as every 5 years, 10 years, or 40 years, and the factors that cause the cycles to change are also diverse. So, you need to have the ability to detect these four seasons of investment in order to play the investment game well. This ability is developed as you repeatedly play the investment game, and it can be maximized through the method of growing your value which will be explained later.

If you participate in the investment game, you can decide the investment target according to the four seasons. People tend to rely on what they see in a situation where they are daunted or feel crisis. Therefore, if the economic situation is bad, cash is concentrated in the value with a high proportion of matter. For example, if a serious crisis occurs, the price of gold and silver increases sharply. On the contrary, if the economy is good, cash is concentrated in the values with a high proportion of imagination such as stocks. Therefore, if you know well about the proportion of matter and imagination of values and how the people feel about the current economic situation, you can easily build a firm standard of investment. When dividing the four seasons of investment into spring-summer-fall-winter, it is summer when the economic situation is the best and it is winter when the situation is the worst. And of course, there are spring and fall between summer and winter.

Spring

In spring, the interest rates are at the lowest point as the cold winter passes and the people's psychology for investment is gradually becoming active. So, it is the time when the liquidity speed of cash is gradually accelerating in the market.

At this time, it is good to invest in the cash flow asset because it is good to utilize the leverage with a low interest rate and it is also easy to find some assets in the market from which the owner couldn't withstand risks during the winter. You can also expect to create cash flow stably in the coming summer. In addition, if you own the cash flow asset in advance, you can lower the risk.

People are paying attention to the cash flow asset or the value growth asset in the spring, but the money is not actively moving and the money tends to be concentrated in the value growth asset a little bit more than the cash flow asset. Therefore, it is easy to find undervalued assets in the cash flow asset class where the value is likely to grow gradually and people are paying less attention.

Summer

In summer, the most value is created and exchanged. In other words, it is the time when the movement of cash is the most active and the price of assets increases rapidly.

At this time, it is good to invest in the value defense asset class. People become aggressive and a lot of cash moves to the asset that will create greater value rather than being used for storing and defending the other values. In other words, money is mostly concentrated in the cash flow asset and the value growth asset. Therefore, assets in the value defense asset class are likely to be undervalued and as a result, it is advantageous to increase your proportion of gold and silver.

Fall

In fall, it is the time when the liquidity speed of cash is gradually slowing down and the interest rate is the highest as the heat of the economic boom, which has peaked, gradually cools down.

At this time, it is better to focus on risk management rather than making investments. It is good to organize the outcomes so far and recharge while lowering the risk level to be prepared for the coming winter.

Winter

In winter, the production of values is very low and the liquidity speed of cash is very slow. In addition, it is the time when the interest rates of loans are going down and people feel the biggest crisis. So, cash is concentrated in the value defense asset class and the price of gold and silver increase.

At this time, it is good to increase your proportion of the value growth asset class because people try to own either cash or the value defense asset rather than the value growth asset for the future with frozen confidence and anxiety. Therefore, there are quite many opportunities to own undervalued assets that may be grown over a relatively long time in winter.

❋ ❋ ❋

Let's take a more straightforward example. The following types of assets are good to acquire for each season of investment.

- Spring: Building for lease, (dividend) stocks
- Summer: Gold and silver
- Fall: Loan repayment

- Winter: Land, stocks

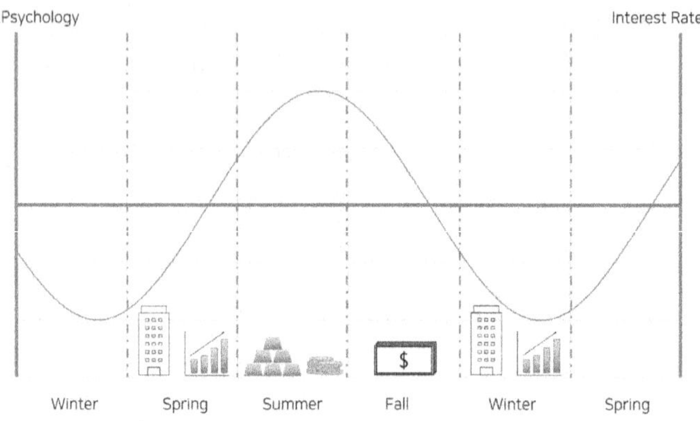

Of course, it doesn't mean that the above standard for investment is absolute, rather it is generally advantageous. Since there are opportunities in all asset classes in every season and people's psychology always appears in a complex manner, it is necessary to have the ability to detect the flow of money well while looking at the market with a wide lens. If you continuously track the changes in values of each asset class and accumulate the asset lists, it would be very helpful. In addition, if you create a source where you can get refined information at any time and develop your intuition to make quick judgments according to the situation, you can flexibly enjoy the investment game.

Special Weather

Phenomena such as typhoons and hurricanes that have a very powerful influence in an instant occur in nature. Similar phenomena occur in the investment game, too. This is often accompanied by a very sudden and unpredictable financial crisis through which diplomatic conflicts or international disputes between major countries, chain bankruptcies of global big companies, or epidemics occur. This kind of massive financial crisis would be a golden opportunity in the investment game.

All financial problems eventually must be solved by cash. And as the crisis gets bigger, economic subjects tend to hold onto cash, not releasing it except for having value defense assets. Therefore, cash is not circulating in the market and the crisis is not easily dissolved. Then, the government must come out to overcome the stagnant economy. They make decisions to make cash flows in the market by using any method possible and it results in an increase in the amount of cash currency in the market. During this period, even if the value of assets does not grow, overvalued assets would come out because the amount of currency increases. The fact that assets move in the direction of overvaluation means that the present is the time for relative undervaluation. Therefore, it is not too much to say that there would be no time when there are more opportunities than this from the side of playing the investment game. So, this period can be called a golden opportunity.

❋ ❋ ❋

We looked at the four seasons of investment. This is necessary to just strategically enjoy investing. So it is better to focus on completing one cycle of investment that involves composing the portfolio as quickly as possible and completing risk management rather than focusing on the four seasons of investment before being qualified to participate in the game. This is because the ability to judge the market situation would be insignificant before participating in the investment game and rather the time to obtain a license for participation would be slowed down due to the restriction in behaviors if you are buried in the long-term flow of the four seasons. Once you start economic activity, you should be able to start the investment game within 10 years. To do so, you must continuously follow the way of growing your own values which will be explained later.

CHAPTER 6. THE MOST POWERFUL VALUE GROWTH ASSETS

I nvestments are made to preserve and grow your own value by replacing it with assets. There are gold and silver representatively in the assets for preserving values and there are various types in the assets for growing values. Let's take a look at the two most powerful types of value growth assets among these. One is real estate and the other is establishment. Since real estate has the matter of space and can contain infinite materials within the space, it can be a powerful value growth asset. In the case of establishment, since it can create infinite value by inputting imagination, it can create the most powerful value growth.

Real Estate

As I emphasized already, you should own the real estate asset as it is the most basic value growth asset. However, it requires more money than other assets, so it is less accessible. And if an investment goes wrong, it is difficult to dispose of it immediately and takes a longer time to exchange with cash.

Just as an object with a large mass has greater gravity in the law of nature, the value also has greater gravity as its size is greater. It is the same as many people gather around those who create great value; many talents gather in a company that creates great value and many customers visit a restaurant that provides great value. In addition, a value with great gravity absorbs other values to grow its own values more. However, in the process of absorbing other values, impurities are inevitably added and such impurities make small cracks. That's why the values that have grown are eventually destroyed or disappear or become smaller again to a certain level. Through this process, the values have a cycle of increasing and decreasing. And this process exactly applies to the real estate's value changes.

The key value of real estate is 'space'. As the space of real estate provides more value, more people gather. Gathering many people means creating more value in that space. In doing so, the valuable space will gradually have greater gravity and it will contain more value in the form of forming commercial districts or building infrastructures such as making new transportation facilities around it. If you think about the process in which cities and markets are formed, it would be easy to understand.

When you own any real estate assets, you should judge the value of the space that the real estate has. I can say that spaces with high values have a good place. It means a good place with solid ground, good quality soil, fine air, good sunlight, and enough water. Major cities around the world are grown on good places. A good place has greater gravity and absorbs more values to grow. People gather, dwellings form, jobs are created, and a commercial district is developed. As infrastructures such as roads and transportation facilities that provide convenience to the people gathered there are built, the value increases more. In this way, real estate that continuously grows value is in a good place. And such good places are good investment targets in real estate.

It is never easy to make investments in real estate. The preparation stage in which to collect the investment funds is not easy and the process of finding, analyzing, and investing in good items is more difficult. Since real estate itself is expensive and requires some degree of expertise in various fields, it is very difficult to reach the level of expert unless you are an investor as a full-time job. So, you need to set standards within the most basic framework and develop your intuition by repeating it. In the investment of real estate, it would be very helpful if you study and experience a lot according to the following standards.

1) The Value of Space

- A site visit is essential. If you have selected a target for investment, you must visit the site first.

- You must focus on the space itself at the site. Feel if the space has the power to attract you in positive way such as comfort or joy.

- Look around the space and at the people around it and try to empathize with how they feel in that space. If you can feel whether people like the space or get vitality, you can judge the value of the space better. It is necessary to look at others as they are with a positive attitude and try to have as much conversation with them as possible.

- Try to estimate the size of gravity the space has. As the gravity is great, the infrastructures such as roads and transportation are well built, and values created by the imagination such as commercial district, jobs and dwellings overlap.

- It is also necessary to check a large range that is difficult to check directly at the site by using a map. This is to feel the values by reflecting on all matters checked directly at the site such as whether it is geographically located well in a wide range or if there are any facilities that may have negative effect on surrounding areas.

2) Changes in Values

- You must judge whether the value of the space is currently increasing or decreasing. Since the growth of value always has a cycle, the value of space can increase or decrease. Therefore, it is more important to judge at what stage the space is at in the cycle of value change rather than the space value at the present time to make the investment.

- Try to check if there are any changes that may affect the value of the space by using all accessible sources such as the news, opinions of experts, and announcements of policy from the government or local government. This is to predict the changes in values through whether there are any plans to build new a commercial district, companies, and dwellings or whether additional infrastructure such as road expansion or transportation facilities may be built.

3) Price Changes

- You must also judge the price apart from the values. Like all assets, the price doesn't always come with the values. And you can get a good chance when the direction of value changes and prices are different in the investment.

- Analyze the price changes of the target. You need to check the price changes by analyzing the changes of the market price in the past and the market price at the present time and judge whether it is a proper price at the present situation.

- Collect and compare all the data that can be checked such as the market price around, the price of other items with a similar form and condition to the target, or the transaction price of other regions with a similar environment.

- Analyze and judge the expected rate of return based on the asset class. For example, the rate of return should be judged by analyzing and predicting whether it can be achieved based on the standards such as more than 10% after 1 year for the cash flow asset and more than 100% after 3 years for the value growth asset.

If you repeat making investments according to these standards, you can have more knowledge and more intuition. At this point, it is important to accept it as it is. When you have a strong desire to make investments, the good things can look better and the bad things can look well, too. When you don't like the target for investment, on the other hand, the good things don't look good and the bad things look worse. That is why you need to maintain a neutral attitude as much as possible when making investments. This ability is also developed through experience.

In my experience, it is difficult to exceed 30% of the investment fund no matter how large the losses are except for in the worst cases such as extremely bad luck or fraud in the investment of real estate. Of course, 30% of the investment fund may be large, but you don't need to think that the loss is just bad since you can gain experience of that equivalence. Therefore, it is necessary to approach to the investment of real estate carefully, but it is also necessary to make investments positively and boldly once the judgment is done.

Lastly, it is good to have advice from the experts when making an investment for the first time. At this point, expert means professionals who provide education and services with a consulting fee, not acquaintances who just know about real estate well and are experienced. The reason why the help of experts is good is that the possibility of failure due to insufficient knowledge and experience is lowered and you can practically learn the knowledge and experience accumulated by experts over a long time in a short period of time. I got to know some experts when I participated in various real estate seminars, and I paid about $6,000 to have consulting for real estate investment to make cash flows. Through just one consultation, I was able to gain the ability to make cash flows that allow me to live only on asset income without labor income by using the investment skills learned from the consultation. And it took less than 2 years to build my whole asset portfolio. If I tried to do everything on my own without the help of experts, it would have taken years or maybe I wouldn't have been able to make it at all.

Establishment

Establishment is surely a flower of investment and multipurpose assets. In terms of value production, all the factors of capital, land, and labor can be put together through establishment. In terms of work, it can do the work of laborers and business owners at the same time. In terms of investment, it is an excellent cash flow asset as well as a powerful value growth asset. In addition, establishment is a life partner who performs your mission together and achieves your vision while doing economic activities in the same form as your own agent. In particular, establishment provides economic benefits to you if it goes well and takes responsibility if it goes wrong. In addition, you can learn about almost every area you encounter as you live the world including the system and organizational structure, judgment of values, economic flows, changes in people's psychology, international relations, asset management and operation, laws, finances, technology, sales and marketing, etc.

Establishment is mostly based on imagination. Therefore, it's variability of values is very high and it continuously depreciates. But the value establishment can hold is almost infinite. Therefore, the constant input of imagination is required for establishment, and if the size of imagination input is large, the establishment grows greater and faster. You can gain riches and fulfill your mission just by exercising the imagination through business, and this is the fastest way to build the structure for a happy life.

The purpose of establishment is to produce and exchange

values. The exchange of values here is mostly made with money. To exchange values, you must produce them first. And you should put produced values into the items so that they can be exchanged well. This means that you should create items to do business.

Items can be created better with more knowledge and experience. You can improve your ability to catch and create values that can be used well in the world while exercising your imagination in the direction of enhancing the parts that are convenient or enjoyable or improving the parts that are inconvenient or bad in your daily life.

Therefore, it is the preparation and beginning of the business to be concerned about every situation you encounter in your daily life and imagine the values that can be created by combining your own knowledge and experiences. Once the business is started, there is no fixed formula or framework. You can just freely operate the business according to your own will and judgment within the boundaries of the laws. Therefore, holding values created with imagination in the actual item is almost everything required to start the business and it takes up more than half of the overall business.

The biggest resistance when establishing business is the fear of failure. You may often see many cases in which people have heavy debt and their life becomes hell because of the failure of business. This is why people tend to have a vague fear of business, but it is relatively easy to dissolve the fear of failure if you consider the fact that the risk always starts with the inability to pay the borrowed money back from an economic point of view. In short, if you don't borrow money when doing business or just borrow money that you can afford to pay back even if the business goes wrong, there is no need to have fear of failure. Some people may say that you can't do business without capital, but there are many ways to start business with little capital by using various platforms such as YouTube or blogs which we can easily access. Or there are also ways to receive investments instead of borrowing money. Or if you operate the business within the limit of saved money from the start, there is no risk because there is no money borrowed even if the business fails. And if the amount of imagination is large, the required capital would be less and it would be also easy to get an investment, having less risk of failure. Therefore, a business in which you input a large proportion of imagination is a better business than the one that requires a lot of capital.

Just like real estate, the greater the value an establishment has, the greater gravity it will have. And if its gravity is getting bigger, it is absorbing more values, making the values grow faster. Here is the difference between real estate and establishment. While real estate stores the value in a fixed space, establishment can easily change the framework that stores the values. This has a significant meaning. No matter how much gravity real estate has, it can't avoid the value changes in which it undergoes stagnation or begins to decrease once its value has grown to some extent. However establishment is different. Of course, there is also a cycle of changes in establishment, but stagnation or degradation of value can be avoided by adding innovative factors to the existing items or changing the business areas. Great corporations with long histories actively utilized the cycle of value changes, for example, by changing their major goods from hardware to software or their industries from manufacturing to service.

Lastly, you can get help from experts on how to invest in establishment, that is, how to do business. From the start, beginning is difficult and there is a high possibility of failure in any area, and it takes a lot of time to accumulate necessary knowledge and experience, so it would be helpful to have help from experts. Experts in business are people who actually operate a good business. Therefore, you can get help from them by having a labor contract with the establishment or doing self-employment with a franchise item. As you work like this, you can learn a lot about business such as what kind of values experts imagined, how they store the value of the item, how to exchange values, how to utilize the cycle of value changes, and how to grow value more. Therefore, experience to work or do self-employment would be very helpful for doing your own business. However, it is better to limit the time to less than 5 years. This is because if it takes more time, your goals can become blurry and you will be likely become controlled by the world.

CHAPTER 7.
USEFUL TOOLS OF INVESTMENT

The most important thing when making investments would be intuition, but you can't rely on your intuition alone for everything. Therefore, you need to utilize tools that help you to make good investments. Some of the useful tools that help you with investment here include financial statements that allow you to check how actual investments are going at a glance and personal connections which will increase the efficiency of investments and supplement areas you can't bear.

Financial Statements

You should know about how your investment is going, how the results are, and what role they plays in your daily life in order to set the direction and make an investment accordingly. Many people write household ledgers to manage incomes and expenditures, but it is not enough to manage investments. If you make a financial statement based on the assets you own, you can manage investments more solidly.

Companies often use a tool called ERP to check and manage

how all of the company's assets and cash are moving. Individuals, like companies, need comprehensive asset management tools and they are especially required for investing. In this case, it is good to use a spreadsheet to increase efficiency.

Personal financial statements should be made in a way that shows the necessary management items based on the assets. The management items are as follows. (It is settled once every month.)

1) Statement of cash flows

- Income: Income is the cash that is paid into your account every month. It is mainly classified and managed into labor income, asset income, and business income.

The reason for dividing labor income and asset income is to be able to easily check whether sufficient income is created as necessary even in a situation where you can't exercise the labor force for some reason.

Business income can include both labor income and asset income depending on the business operation method, but it is better to separately classify them since it has a relatively high variability in income.

Numbers for the income item are entered by dividing the expected deposit amount and date and the actual deposit amount and date.

- Expenditure: Expenditure is the cash that is drawn out of your account. It can be expressed as a cost. Expenditure is classified and managed by fixed costs and variable costs. Fixed costs are the ones that are not affected by the changes in income, and variable costs are the ones that change according to a change in income.

Fixed costs include food expenses, communication expenses, housing expenses (utility bills), loan interests, personnel expenses, transportation expenses, and insurance. Variable costs include taxes representatively.

As a detailed item for expenditure, donation, savings, and entertainment expenses can be managed as a fixed cost with a fixed amount of money each month or they can be managed as a variable cost by setting a proportion. However it is better to manage them as a variable cost. This is because if labor income accounts for most of the income, there would be no big difference whether they are managed as a fixed cost or a variable cost, but it would be easy to manage income and expenditure as the asset income and business incomes that have relatively high variability are added.

You may not say that the taxes and savings are expenditures that are drawn out of the account every month, but they are expenses that are accumulated for a certain period and are eventually consumed. So, they are managed as expenditure items.

Just like income, expenditures are also entered by dividing the expected expenditure and date and the actual expenditure and date. In the case of expected date, for example, if there is a date of fixed expenditure such as a card payment or rental fee, it is necessary to regularly check the items with the upcoming date to prevent them from being overdue.

It can be made in the following way.

Statement of Cash Flows

Income					
Category 1	Category 2	Expected		Actual		Remarks
		Amount	Date	Amount	Date	
Asset Income	Real Estate					
	Dividend					
Sum				(a)		
Labor Income	Labor Contract					
Sum				(b)		
Business Income	Biz. 1					
	Biz. 2					
Sum				(c)		
Total				(d)		

Highlights		
Asset Income Ratio	(a)/(d)	%
Business Income Ratio	(c)/(d)	%
Surplus	(d) - (e)	₩
Rate of Surplus Change		%

Expenditure					
Category 1	Category 2	Expected		Actual		Remarks
		Amount	Date	Amount	Date	
Fixed	Housing					
	Insurance					
	Loan Interest 1					
	Loan Interest 2					
Variable	Donation					
	Saving					
	Loan Repayment					
	Taxes					
Total				(e)		

Accumulated Money		
Saving		₩
Loan Repayment		₩
Taxes		₩

- If you separate the proportion of expected amount and actual amount of income and expenditure, it would be easy to check whether the cash flow management is working as planned.

- More than 10% of the income should be saved for investment and more than 20% should be paid back for the loan. This is the most basic preparation and management for the investment. If there are no assets and loans at first, more than 30% in total should be saved.

- The amount deducted total expenditure from the total expenditure is the surplus. The surplus can be used freely to purchase luxury goods, to add to a trip or portfolio, or to manage the risk (repayment of loan). Making such surplus large is the key in the management of the cash flow table. A representative way to explosively increase the surplus is the success of business and the sale of value growth assets at lower level. Even though it is not that much, the acquisition of cash flow asset also increases the surplus.

- It is not easy to accurately calculate taxes since taxes increase as the size of assets increases, so it is necessary to prepare for taxes by saving in advance after estimating them as accurately as possible with the help of an accountant to avoid any problems with the cash flow.

2) Asset status table

A detailed status of all the assets you currently own is managed through the asset status table. This asset status table is the key to the financial statement.

It can be made in the following form.

Asset Status Table

Asset										
No.	Class	Type	Name	Date of Acquisition	Acquisition Price	Acquisition Cost	Asset Price(estimated)	Total Amount of Loan	Net Asset Price	Loan-Net Price Ratio	Risk Level
1	Self	Credit									
2	Self	Insurance									
3	Currency	USD									
4	Currency	EURO									
5	Basic	House									
6	Cash Flow	Real Estate 1									
7	Cash Flow	Real Estate 2									
8	Cash Flow	Stock 1									
9	Cash Flow	Stock 2									
10	Value Growth	Real Estate 3									
11	Value Growth	Stock 3									
12	Value Growth	Stock 4									
13	Value Defense	Gold									
14	Value Defense	Silver									

Contract										
No.	Class	Type	Name	Start Date	End Date	Contract Amount	Interest Rate	Period	Income/Payment Amount	Transaction Date	Asset No.
1	Self	Loan	xxx credit loan				2%	Monthly			1
2	Basic	Loan	xxx mortgage loan				2.50%	Monthly			5
3	Cash Flow	Loan	xxx mortgage loan				2.70%	Monthly			6
4	Cash Flow	Loan	xxx mortgage loan				2.20%	Monthly			7
5	Cash Flow	Loan	xxx deposit				0%	N/A			8
6	Cash Flow	Profit	xxx rent				N/A	Weekly			6
7	Cash Flow	Profit	xxx dividend				N/A	Quarterly			8

Highlights	
Total Asset Price(estimated))	
Total Amount of Loan	
Total Net Asset Price(estimated)	

Asset Portfolio				
Class	Net Asset Price	Proportion	Appropriate Rate	Integrity
Basic			30%	
Cash Flow			35%	
Value Growth			25%	
Value Defense			10%	

Risk Management Plan (Loan Repayment)						
Order	Class	Appropriate Rate	Actual Rate	Risk Level	Interest Rate	Contract No.
1	Self	5%	20%	400%	2%	1
2	Basic	20%	40%	200%	2.50%	2
3	Cash Flow	75%	90%	120%	2.70%	3
4	Cash Flow	75%	90%	120%	2.20%	4
5						
6						
7						

- Link the status of contracts such as loans or leases for each asset in order to manage them well. Check the items that have upcoming expiration dates in advance through regular checking. This way, you should be able to prepare plans for a contract renewal or new contracts.

- The expected price at the present time is the amount that it is expected to be sold at. Since the price changes in real time, it is necessary to check it with a certain cycle. If you judge as accurately as possible based on all available data and information, you can compose an accurate portfolio and manage the risk.

- Portfolio management: Check the proportion of assets entered in the asset status table based on the asset class and net assets and manage them in a direction to increase integrity.

- Risk management: Check the amount of loans among the assets entered in the asset status table based on the standard of asset classes and manage them in a direction to reduce risk at an appropriate level.

You must set a date every month to settle how your cash flows have moved and what changes have been made in the asset status, and then make a plan for how to manage your assets and investments for the next month. Such management using financial tool helps you a lot for good investing. In addition, you can develop the ability to exercise control on the value you own.

Personal Connections

Since the amount of knowledge and information required for investment is too vast, it is almost impossible to do everything on your own. So, just like you utilize the leverage in an investment by borrowing money, you can also use knowledge and information as leverage. This can be referred to as human leverage and it can shorten the time and increase the quality of the investment.

Human leverage is to get help from other people. To do so, you need to build good personal connections. If you get the help from experts for investments, those experts can be your personal connection, and the relationships you make in the process of making investments also can be personal connections.

Suppose you are making an investment in a real estate asset. At first, you need to select a nearby or certain area and visit a brokerage office there since you have no personal connections. Or you might try to find an expert by searching and know the investment target. You start to build your personal connections in this way and expand your connections to various ranges such as judicial scriveners, tax accountants, people in charge of bank loans, interior agencies, etc. during all processes that follow. In this way, the investment and making personal connections are made together and as you repeat with more investments, your connections widen and become stronger. As a result, it allows you to have good helpers in the right places and gradually make successful investments.

At first, you have no choice but to start with no personal connections. As you meet new people and make personal connections, connection management begins, but it is very difficult to judge what level of value they can provide. Again, let's set up and imagine the situation of investing in real estate. It would start with meeting a broker. Just as it is difficult to judge the value of a broker from the standpoint of investing, it is also difficult for a broker to judge the value of investors whom they meet for the first time. People often don't provide all of the information when they don't know each other. Therefore, it is almost impossible to get a good item from a broker whom you meet for the first time. However, as you undergo the process of investing and making actual transactions, you can judge each other's values. If you think that the value of a broker is high, you will want to continue the transaction with that broker, and that broker also will introduce a better item if he/she thinks that you provide enough values. When personal connections are becoming solid in this way, you will introduce related people including judicial scriveners, tax accountants, people in charge of bank loans, interior agents, etc. to each other and the personal connections are expanded. Expanded connections become more solid and, each connection is built through a circular structure that expands to another connection.

It is very important to build personal connections, but this doesn't mean that you should create and manage the connections intentionally. You will have a good impression on those who provide true values to you. You will naturally keep in touch and meet with those whom you have a good impression, and you might want to give more values to them. In this process, personal connections are naturally built, maintained, and expanded. In the end, if you treat people with a positive mind and gratitude for the value they give, you will naturally build and manage your own personal connections well.

PART IV. DAY

Since my life has changed, many people ask me how to make money. My answer is always the same: what they really want. And their answers are always the same: they want to retire as soon as possible and live comfortably without worrying about having to work. Most of our conversations always go like this.

Other person: "How can I make money? What kind of investment should I make?"

Me: "What do you want to do by investing?"

Other person: "I just hope I can earn money equal to my salary and not work."

Me: "That is what you don't want to do. I mean what you want to do."

Other person: "I can't say anything specifically, but I wish I would feel comfortable without getting stress from work."

Me: "Hmm, then get up two hours earlier than you do now. And meditate and read books."

Other person: "All I know is that I can't get up early."

Me: "What if you could be rich only if you can get up early?"

Other person: "Then I can do that."

Me: "Yeah, you can be rich if you get up early. So, try that first. There are many things to do other than meditation and reading. I will tell you everything."

Other person: "Anything more practical than that? Like where and how much I should invest?"

Me: "I found a good investment seminar. Do you want to go? It costs $500."

Other person: "It's too expensive. I need to think about it."

Most conversations are similar. In the end, we just need to be happier than we are now and gradually we'll become happy. However people focus on money too much. I'm convinced that if money itself becomes the purpose, it would be very difficult and take very long to make that money. And they won't be happy even after making as much money as they initially targeted. But if we pursue happiness, money that fits the size of happiness naturally comes along.

Anyone can make as much money as they return in value to the world by accepting a lot of it and adding their own value. If so, they can just think and act accordingly. There are countless ways to make money and invest in the world. We just need to find a way that suits our tendencies. What's really important is to accept a lot of values, create our own values, and return a lot of values to the world.

There is only one person who listened to me and followed my advice among all of those who had this type of conversation with me. Not long after he started taking action, he went down the path to happiness. He bought a house, made a good relationship, and is becoming happier while gradually doing what he really wants.

CHAPTER 1. SEIZE THE DAY

I have explained the concepts and some ways required to live a happy life so far, but no matter how good of goals and plans you have, it would be useless if you don't execute them. You must set the direction, create practical values, and accumulate them. And it is only today that you can do this because you can't live the past again and the future has not yet come. After all, how much value you grow today and how constantly you repeat such days determines how quickly you will go in the way of happiness.

Let's take an example to emphasize the importance of execution. There would be many people who have a short temper and don't understand other's feelings among the successful people you can see around. In addition, there would be many people who have bad personalities or are evaluated as morally bad. That is why people tend to think that living while being good will not make any success, but this is wrong. Those kinds of people are more likely to succeed because they have advantageous personalities to execute what they want without any hesitation. If they have the same executive power, the person who has a high morality among them will succeed much more.

Anyway, execution is very important, but here is the problem. You may know that you can make a good plan to execute.

However the problem is that it is always difficult to execute it and it is more difficult to execute it constantly. This is because of inertia and resistance. Inertia and resistance are not just occurring in natural phenomena. There are also inertia and resistance in your mind. It would be easier to understand if you think of values as objects with mass and area. In natural phenomena, when the mass of an object is large, the inertia also becomes large, and when the area is large, the resistance becomes also large. It is same for values. People feel greater inertia and resistance as they do more valuable things. That is why it is hard to start valuable things and it is even harder to keep doing them. For example, opening books is hard, but turning the TV on is easy. When you watch TV, it may not be hard or boring to watch simple entertainment programs for a long time, but you'd probably get easily tired when watching educational programs. Let's look at it the other way around. The things you don't want to do and are difficult to keep are more valuable for you. You need to understand the natures of the value to execute things. And you need to utilize most of the inertia and try to find ways to reduce resistance.

In this section, I will just explain about the execution of accumulating additional values while living each day except for the usual workday from morning to afternoon based on the daily life of general laborers because some degree of compulsion must be imposed to continuously accumulate values during the workday.

You must create routines to constantly execute valuable work. The thought of doing valuable work itself is also valuable, so you encounter inertia and resistance to stopping from the process of having such thought. You also encounter inertia and resistance to stopping in the process of doing actual action. So, when you come up with something valuable every moment and try to execute it, it is difficult to even get started. And even if you can do it for the first few times, it is very difficult to maintain it. This is why short-lives resolutions are very common. For this reason, it is good to make a routine of valuable things as a bundle and reduce the stage of thinking, and this will reduce the inertia of stopping and resistance, too.

The placement of the routine is also important, and it is good to execute the most important routines early in the morning. To be precise, it is good to start the day with the most important routine. Many people will think, 'It would be better to do valuable things in the evening because I can't get up in the morning well and I can focus more in the evening because I'm a typical evening person,' but if you try to do something in the evening after finishing the day's work, your mental and physical energy are already mostly consumed, so it is difficult to do something valuable, and you once again encounter the inertia of stopping and resistance on the way to starting. That is why it is good to place the most important routine into the daily work that you naturally do without having to think about it as soon as you open your eyes in the morning.

I will explain how to use inertia now. You may have some experience that has helped you to be able to continue doing something with less difficulty than you thought once you started doing it, no matter how difficult it was and unwilling to do it you were. This is because inertia occurred in the direction of moving. And you should know about concentration. According to brain science, a person can only concentrate for 15 to 20 minutes on one subject. In addition, concentration can be increased when you feel a bit of pressure. These natures can be used well. When you do something, you can start it by setting a timer for 15 minutes. Since there is a time limit of 15 minutes, you feel a bit of pressure and your concentration can become increased. After 15 minutes when the timer goes off, you have inertia on the things you have stared and are able to continue a little longer. In the end, you can do one thing while maintaining a high level of concentration for about 15-20 minutes.

As such, if you make the most valuable things into a routine, start the day with that routine, and use inertia with a high level of concentration by the help of a timer, you can create a day that accumulates as many values as possible efficiently and repeatedly. Even if you use this method, the matter of execution might still remain difficult. However, I'm sure that there are no better ways than this and you will feel that it is worth being done if you try it once.

CHAPTER 2. TOOLS FOR VALUE GROWTH

Now, let's find out the specific ways to grow your values. There are many ways for self-improvement in the world. I will introduce the way that worked the best for me among them. If you create your own routine by using this as a tool and place it in your daily work, you will certainly make very efficient value growth.

Reading

Reading is the best tool to build value. Books are the outcome of value reproduced by adding imagination to the value authors have obtained from the world over a long time. In other words, books are well-refined collections of values. Therefore, you can efficiently obtain high quality values created by something through reading.

There are countless kinds of books in the world and one book has about 300 pages on average. And it takes about 3.5 hours on average to read this length of books. This means that you can obtain high quality values which the author devoted to writing while experiencing, thinking, and organizing for a long time in just 3.5 hours. It is said that one must read at least 100 books in related fields to write one book. Therefore, the time efficiency that can be obtained through reading is more than 100 times that of direct experience. In other words, you can obtain a large amount of value materials in a short time. In addition, reading enables you to transcend the physical, periodical, and spatial limitations of direct experience. For example, it allows you to indirectly experience and imagine the areas that can't be directly experienced such as historical events in the past or natural phenomena that appear on the other side of the earth.

You must intake nutrients for your body to grow and to maintain your health. The three most basic nutrients are protein, carbohydrates, and fats. Likewise, you must intake valuable materials to grow and maintain your value, and the most basic way to take in these materials is by reading. Here, the fields of books that can be compared to the three nutrients are 'philosophy', 'history', and 'literature'.

Just as protein builds muscles and makes them strong, philosophy makes your value itself strong. Philosophy covers all of the essences of the world and analyzes which matters are composed of value and how imagination is applied in depth.

Just as carbohydrates provide direct energy for people to move, history develops the ability to apply imagination to materials. History tells you how materials are combined and used with imagination and how the outcome worked out.

Lastly, just as fats help with generating hormones to grow the body, literature creates the hormone that develops the ability for imagination. Literature shows the limits of the imagination to create a virtual world by exercising the imagination beyond the real world and freely combining and reorganizing value materials.

In addition to these, there are books in other various fields such as society, economy, politics, science, technology, culture, and art. If you make a firm foundation of value through philosophy, history, and literature, the value you can accumulate through books in other fields will be greater. Therefore, you must grow your own value while building a solid foundation with philosophy, history, and literature as well as reading books in other various fields. In general, if you read a total of 1,000 books, including 200 philosophy books, 100 history books, 300 literary books, and 400 books in other fields, you will cross certain thresholds and create a very good bundle of values.

From a brain science perspective, the time your brain can concentrate on one subject does not exceed 20 minutes. And even when switching to a different subject, your brain organizes the subject you focused on before in the unconscious area. You can make good use of this point which is to increase the efficiency of reading while reading various types of books at the same time. For example, you can prepare 1 book each from philosophy, history, and literature and alternatively read them in a cycle of 15 – 20 minutes. In my experience, it was the most efficient when I read 3 books for a total of 45 minutes to 1 hour by setting a timer for 15 minutes for each book. If you do like this, the time devoted to one book is less than 20 minutes, which is not a large amount of reading. So, it is easy to take note of sentences or content that is important or needs to be remembered.

Just like eating and taking nutrients every day, you must read every day. It is good to read for at least 1 hour a day and, in doing so, you can obtain values from about 100 books per year. If you start reading while your reading volume is not much, sometimes you can't understand the content no matter how much you focus on it. So, you may feel that the effect of reading is not great and that you just spend time at the level of accepting only texts. This is mostly because you may be not familiar with the terminology and have no sufficient background knowledge. But when reading volume is accumulated, this is naturally solved. Therefore, it's better to focus on securing the reading volume first.

Newspaper

Newspapers are also a very powerful and essential tool to grow values. While reading was compared to nutrients, especially the three major nutrients, reading newspapers can be compared to vitamins. Just as vitamins activate each function of your body, newspapers infuse life into each area of the values you've accumulated.

Newspapers tell you what's happening at the present time in all the areas you encounter while living such as the economy, politics, society, international relations, technology, culture, art, and history. You can know how imagination deals with materials in all areas of the world through newspapers.

Reading newspapers is like looking at the history of the world microscopically. It is important to catch how history changes over time. Therefore, continuity is important when reading newspapers and you must read newspapers every day like books. You must read newspapers for as long as possible to feel the current of the times, meaning you need to read newspapers constantly for at least 3 months. After that, you start to have and feel a sense of connectivity between articles in different areas.

Paper newspapers are better than electronic/digital newspapers. (It's the same for all reading materials including books.) This is because there are fatal drawbacks in electronic newspapers. First, you can feel tired because the speed of reading and scrolling are different in the form of electronic newspapers, so you often don't read the sentences properly. Second, if you need to scroll back and check the content that's passed by, it is difficult to find its location, making you easily give up on finding it. Third, you can feel more bored than the paper format because it is difficult to intuitively notice how much you have read in the length of the entire content. In addition, the order and sizes are different depending on the importance of the articles in the newspaper. However the electronic format can't express this, so it is difficult to notice more important articles whether consciously or unconsciously and you feel more bored. And there is a comment section, too, which makes you focus on comments rather than the main articles. For these reasons, it is much better to subscribe to paper newspapers than electronic ones in order to read the newspaper properly.

Just like books, you need to read newspapers in a good way. First is to distinguish the facts from the opinions. Newspaper articles are often interpreted and expressed in different ways depending on the press or reporters, even for the same materials. This is why you must distinguish the facts from the opinions when reading a newspaper. It would be helpful for extracting facts if you carefully check the source and citations of the materials when reading articles. For example, if there is content including the announcement of the government or a company, it is a fact. On the other hand, if there is content including interviews or analysis of experts or scholars on the announcement, it is an opinion. Second is to grasp the important issues. It is good to use the first page and editorial and column parts to grasp the important issues. This is because the first page, of course, deals with the most important issues of the day and the editorial or columns normally deal with the topics which are the important issues. If you keep these two in mind, you can initially read the first page carefully, then read all of the editorials and then columns and then read topics that interest you while checking all of the titles for the rest of the articles and then just read the titles or roughly look at the content for the rest. In this way, you can read a newspaper efficiently within about 30-40 minutes.

Seminar

A seminar is like supplementary nutrients because it intensively fills the parts that can't be fully conveyed in a book or newspaper on a specific topic in a short time. There are various forms like a conference or lecture that have similar characteristics to a seminar, but I will refer to them all as a seminar in this book.

A seminar is a way to accumulate necessary value in the shortest time in your current situation. In particular, it would be great help when you have a purpose for learning practical investment, not just obtaining knowledge. It is a very good tool for learning information and technology that can be applied and used right away and for building personal connections.

A seminar progresses from one hour to tens of hours on a specific topic. Since a seminar is held for various topics and forms regardless of region, it is very easy to find seminars about the parts you want to fill in or values that you want to have. For example, there are seminars with the purpose of conveying knowledge covering relatively wide ranges such as economy, finance, marketing, writing, history, humanities, and psychology, and there are seminars for telling you about technologies that are specific and can be applied right away such as how to use SNS, stock investment skills, auctions, and even how to read newspapers well. If you participate in a seminar which you feel is interesting or you think it is necessary after finding it regularly in the range of areas you can access, you will grow your own value very efficiently.

An off-line seminar is better than an online seminar, but there are also high quality seminars online. Therefore, you don't need to stick to off-line only. In my experience, it is appropriate to devote about 2-4 hours to participate in seminars per month on average while constantly reading books and newspapers.

Writing

The purpose of growing your own value is to fulfill your mission by providing value to the world in the end. To provide your own value well, the values must be well refined, otherwise, it is difficult to provide values, and it is also difficult to use it for those who accept them. In particular, well-refined values are essential factors to create items well in the business. A well-refined value can be referred to as a value with a high resolution.

The best way to increase the resolution of value is writing. Writing can be compared to exercise. Exercise uses nutrients you took to make your body strong. Likewise, writing increases the purity of value materials you have and makes your imagination solid. As a result, a firm value with high resolution can be created.

The efficiency of learning appears differently depending on the methods, and one of the cited data is the 'Learning Pyramid Model' published by the National Training Laboratories. There is some controversy over its reliability, but intuitionally it seems to have enough data to agree with. According to the learning pyramid model, 'teaching' has the best efficiency of the learning methods. Writing is the outcome that comes out after having the processes of reading, listening, seeing, researching, thinking, organizing, and revising. This process can be applied equally to the teaching. In other words, writing is to teach with a tool called writing. Therefore, writing is a way to increase the resolution of value and is the best method in terms of learning efficiency at the same time.

There are also some good things about writing. The first one is to that you get to use your brainwave cycle. You need to use as much imagination as possible when writing and you need to have help from your unconscious mind. The brainwave cycles that can get the help of the unconscious are the 'Theta' and 'Alpha' wave cycles. Among them, the alpha wave cycle can be applied practically. One of the most common ways to create the alpha wave cycle while doing daily life is to take a shower with warm water. Therefore, it is good to think about writing while taking a shower. You can think about various things when you take a shower, and your imagination can be exercised by just thinking about writing, and sentence expressions often appear in the mind. As such, you can use brainwave cycle by organizing the chunk of imagination appeared while taking shower in writing after finishing the shower.

WAVE	STATUS
DELTA (0.1 ~ 4Hz)	Deep Sleep
THETA (4 ~ 8Hz)	Creative State, Drowsiness
ALPHA (8 ~ 12Hz)	Relaxed Focus, Daydreaming
SMR (12 ~ 15Hz)	Body Calmness, Mental Alertness
BETA (15 ~ 20Hz)	Active Thinking, Problem Solving
HIGH BETA (20Hz ~)	Excited, Irritability

The second is to use tools such as a 'Mind Map' or 'Visual Thinking'. These organize your thoughts or topics simply and create a basic framework, increasing resolution. If you use these tools to increase resolution first and then write, you can concentrate better and be able to avoid getting off topic.

The third is the length of writing. You should write at least 400 words to organize the background to some extent and draw conclusions. And as the chunk of thoughts gets bigger, the length of writing should become longer. And if the writing is long, it is difficult to organize and it is easier to get off topic. Therefore, it is necessary to set a minimum length of writing and practice to place and combine content according to the framework. As you become familiar with writing, you may feel that 400 words is not enough to express all of your thoughts.

The last one is about the writing cycle. As advised, if you read books for about 1 hour a day, read newspapers for more than 30 minutes a day, and participate in seminars once or twice a month, the materials for writing will be easily accumulated. Based on the book, you can read 2-3 books on average in 2 weeks and you can finish at least 1 book even if you read 3 books for 15 minutes each at the same time. Therefore, you can have a good cycle if you do writing once every 2 weeks. If you set a time for 1 hour once every 2 weeks and write a book report or essay, it will be very helpful in increasing the resolution of the values you have.

Meditation

When you accept values from outside and store them as material, impurities are always mixed with prejudice and subjective judgment. For example, people tend to listen carefully when someone they like and respect speaks about something and try to accept it as much as possible. On the other hand, people tend to not listen carefully to someone they don't like and underestimate their speaking and try to find errors. Of course, you need to comprehensively understand behaviors and the background of the person speaking when you listen to them. However, such judgment should be made after accepting what the person is saying as it is. Meditation helps eliminate impurities that are mixed when accepting values in this respect.

The basis of meditation is that it is a practice of accept things as they are. It is to feel the present as it is and to accept external and internal feelings occurring at the present time as they are. It is to feel and accept what your eyes see, what your ears hear, what your skin feels, and any current feelings and thoughts as they are. Mediation is a practice of accurately recognizing current feelings, and you must accept the values given by the world and the inner changes as they are through the practice of meditation. If you accept values from outside without any impurities, you can see the value clearly. And you can better understand about what matters and imagination the values you have accepted consist of and you can also judge the size of the value reasonably. It works the same for the values created from inside. And if you feel your mind purely, it would be helpful to understand what you really want. Meditation is not something that ends after feeling the effect and gaining the peace of mind at the moment. It is something to practice in your daily life so that you can accept the present as it is.

Mediation works best when it is silent because you can easily be complex and lose your concentration if there are many things to feel. There are many ways to do meditation. One good way is to expand the area of feelings by dividing them. First, choose a silent time. Sit in a comfortable position, close your eyes, and concentrate on your senses. And expand your senses from the outside to in while feeling them. For example, you can feel the sound through your ears and concentrate on the sensation on the skin while keeping those senses. And then you can expand your senses to smell the air you breathe with your nose, feeling the air entering your lungs, you heart beat and your blood circulating. And the last is to expand the area through the way to feel emotions and thoughts. If feels like seeing through your body and mind with your spirit after separating your spirit from your body.

Only when you keep this state of mediation for more than 15 minutes, will it have the effects of practice. In addition, since meditation can't bring remarkable outcomes in a short period of time, you must keep doing it for a long time in order to train and practice accepting things as they are during your daily life.

Morning Exercise

There is a saying that goes 'sound body, sound mind'. Strengthening the body which is the appearance of your asset is like making a solid frame to store value. You must have a living habit to maintain your health through exercise.

Morning exercise is especially effective in various ways. It takes some time for your brain and body to be fully activated after waking up. And morning exercise speeds up the pace. So, it eliminates the thoughts of wanting to fall asleep again and it makes it easy to do the next part of your morning routine. This also helps with developing a positive mind and confidence.

It is good to do morning exercise to the point where you are out of breath slightly, not just at the level of simply stretching. It is for the effect obtained other than health. Exercises suitable for this purpose are weight training such as squats or pushups and aerobic exercises such as running. I think that squats are the best because they are not limited by space, no special preparation is required, they strengthen the muscles, and their effect on blood circulation is very excellent. Normally 5 minutes is enough to squat around 60-120 times by dividing them into sets. 5-minute exercises every morning are a way to increase value with high efficiency by getting effects such as health for both body and mind as well as inertia to spend the day well. Drinking a glass of water after morning exercise is more effective.

Sleep

If your quality of sleep is low or time is insufficient, you can become helpless, tired, and vulnerable to stress, and it may increase the possibility to have a negative mindset. As a result, it would be difficult to spend your day in a worthwhile manner. Therefore, you need to get a good sleep plan to have worthwhile day.

To increase the quality of sleep, you should use the cycle of brain activity well. The cycle of sleep determined depending on the cycle of brain activity. Sleep can be divided into light sleep and deep sleep. It is good to wake up from a light sleep cycle when waking up in the morning. When you wake up at dawn, you may experience not feeling tired and your mind is clear, even though you didn't sleep much. On the other hand, there are times when you are strangely tired and it feels hard to get up even though the entire length of sleep was long. This may be because when waking up at dawn for a moment, it was the time of a light sleep cycle, and when waking up after sleeping for a long time, it was time for a deep sleep cycle. Sleep is repeated in one cycle of 'light sleep – deep sleep – light sleep', and research shows that a cycle usually takes about 90 minutes. Therefore, it is good to sleep within periods of 90 minutes such as the units of 1.5 hours, 3 hours, 4.5 hours, 6 hours, and 7.5 hours.

The length of sleeping time is also important. According to research, it is good to sleep between 7 and 8 hours. In my experience, a 5-time sleep cycle was the best. In other words, it is good to sleep for 7.5 hours. When I did that, I wasn't tired for the day and was able to fully concentrate on valuable work with a positive mind. When you spend a day by enjoying simple pleasures without doing something worthwhile, there would be no problems even if you slept for 6 hours, 4.5 hours, or even 3 hours. However, you need 7.5 hours of sleeping time to activate the brain properly and have a day that grows your value effectively. Since the cycle may vary depending on individual, you need to observe your own sleeping cycle and try to optimize it.

It may difficult to have 7.5 hours when you are actively involved in economic activities. In this case, it is recommended to sleep for an additional 20 minutes at the time of feeling tired while having a basic sleeping time such as 6 hours. The reason for having a basis as 20 minutes is that it is the time before switching to a deep sleep from a light sleep, and fatigue felt when waking up from a deep sleep can be avoided.

Sometimes you may not fall asleep easily. Sleeping also requires good method and practice. In this case, it is good to use brain waves, too. Staying away from electronic devices such as smartphones 30 minutes before falling asleep and meditating 15 minutes before sleeping will change your brain waves into 'Alpha' waves and help you fall asleep easily. If you meditate while lying down, it is easy to fall asleep with a comfortable mind and you can also practice meditating until you fall asleep. That is the effect of killing two birds with one stone.

Once you set your sleeping time, you can know what time to fall asleep based on the time of waking up. It means if you fix the time to wake up according to your routines, you can also fix the time to go to sleep. Therefore, if you fix the sleeping time, you can create a regular lifestyle pattern that helps a lot for growing your values.

Making the Bed

Making the bed in the morning is probably one of the most common things, but it is thought of as the least effective thing among many ways for self-improvement. Many self-help books say that you can obtain achievements by doing something, even if it is very small like making the bed, and it makes you start the day with success. That helps you to develop your self-esteem. Yes, it's true, but I would like to say that there are more practical advantages in addition to these effects. First, if you set making the bed as a task you must do as soon as you wake up in the morning, it is certainly easier to wake up in the morning. Usually you don't easily get up because of the inertia of sleeping when you wake up from sleeping. In addition, you try to find reasons to sleep more while thinking of what to do. At this point, if there is something that must be done without having any special thoughts, and if it is making the bed which is not that difficult, you can greatly reduce your difficulties when waking up in the morning. Second, making the bed has the effect of waking up a brain that is not completely awake. To make the bed, you need to adjust the angles to some extent, and at this time, you need a little concentration. And the slight mental exercise of concentration provides the effect to activate the brain. The last one is the effect of inertia. In terms of activity, sleeping has the inertia of stopping and getting up and moving have the inertia of moving. Making the bed makes you have the inertia of moving and creates inertia to easily start the task or routine that you must do next.

If you have no environment for making the bed, just place a towel nearby which you can fold in the morning after you wake up. And keep in mind that if you fold the towel while laying down, it would be difficult to have the same effect as making bed; therefore you should fold it while standing.

Goal Writing

It is said that if you write the goal you wish to achieve 100 times a day, then that goal will come true. I refer to this as 100 times writing or goal writing. The working principle of goal writing is to imprint your wishes into your subconscious while writing it repeatedly to make you think and act in the direction of fulfilling the wishes even if you are not conscious of it in your daily life, and then eventually to make it come true.

Once you find your mission and set a vision, you can determine the goals to be specifically achieved. If you choose one of them and write your goals 100 times a day for 100 days, it will be a great help for you to achieve your vision.

Goal writing will have an effect only when you concentrate as much as possible and carefully write it while imagining it coming true. That is why silent time with less external interference is good for goal writing.

To be specific, I suggest you write three goals in a year. It is to write one goal every 4 months like January to April, May to August, and September to December. If you do this, there would be some days when you aren't able to do it. So, you can write one wish 100 times a day for about 100 to 120 days. And the sentence structure could be like 'when + what + how', for example, 'In *year* + 1 kg of gold + store in portfolio'. It will take about 25 to 30 minutes to write one sentence 100 times.

Morning Diary

A diary is a great tool to remember and store the values received from the world. Writing a diary in the morning works better. After sleeping, many of the experiences you have in a day are forgotten, and only the most impressive or important events are likely to remain in your memory. Therefore, if you write a dairy in the morning, you can organize and record the events that are considered the most important among the experiences from yesterday.

You can write a dairy with simple short sentences in a total of 4 categories. First, write 3 things about good experiences such as an event you felt good about or impressed by the day before. Second, write 3 things about any bad experiences such as events where you felt uncomfortable, irritated, or bad the day before. Third, write the 3 most important things to be completed among your tasks on "today" (that day). Last, write 3 wishes that are likely to occur or you want to happen with other people's help or environmental conditions regardless of your will on "today" (that day). It will take about 10-15 minutes to write 12 simple and short sentences. During this time, you can wrap up the experiences you had yesterday and feel a sense of achievement and gratitude about the completion of tasks and the realization of wishes.

Gratitude and Donation

If you live your life with a truly positive attitude, you will be grateful every moment. This is because people receive endless values and help from the world every second. And if you have true gratitude for the world, you will also have a positive attitude. Therefore, if you become more positive, you will feel more gratitude, and if your gratitude gets bigger, you will be more positive. In this way, positiveness and gratitude have a structure that gradually grows while circulating.

This is why you must create a virtuous cycle of positiveness and gratitude. Compared to positiveness, gratitude is more specific and easier to develop. Positiveness can be developed by taking care of your usual attitude or doing meditation, but it will take a lot of time to get a noticeable outcome. In particular, you need to care for and focus on whether you have a positive attitude at every moment and judge whether it is an appropriate action to have a positive mind and practice it in daily life. But it is quite difficult to take care of every moment and it consumes too much energy. On the other hand, there are ways to develop gratitude by repeating specific behaviors. In other words, gratitude can be developed easily compared to positiveness and it is easy to make a virtuous structure of positiveness and gratitude through this.

To have a mind of feeling true gratitude, if you repeat a behavior that will naturally follow when you are grateful intentionally, you can have a good effect. There are two ways which are to express gratitude and to make donations.

The first one is the expression of gratitude. You can just look back on the day after finalizing it before falling asleep and express gratitude to the world. The easiest way is to pray. If you follow a religion, you can pray according to it, and otherwise, you can set a certain target like 'the eight guiding princes' mentioned by Napoleon Hill in *YOU CAN WORK YOUR OWN MIRACLES* to pray.

At this time, you need something to be thankful for to pray. But if you repeat doing this every day, you will be forced to make up such things and it will easily give up due to the pain of having to create it. So, it is good to set a thing to be thankful for in advance. And it would be very good to make your own prayer and recite it before going to sleep. You can refer to 'the eight guiding princes' (Financial Prosperity, Sound Physical Health, Peace of Mind, Hope, Faith, Love, Romance, and Overall Wisdom) of Napoleon Hill to make a great prayer for gratitude. You can read *YOU CAN WORK YOUR OWN MIRACLES* by Napoleon Hill or find it easily through the Internet. If you recite your prayer while thinking about your experiences of the day as images before going to bed every night, you will gradually have true gratitude.

Donation, which is the second way, is simpler. Donation is the easiest and most efficient way to have true gratitude. This is because you can simply give money. However when this simple act is repeated, gratitude is imprinted in your mind. 10% of your monthly income would be appropriate for a donation. This is because 10% of your income is never small when judging based on financial statements. On the other hand, it is an amount that doesn't significantly interfere with making investments or operating living expenses. If 10% of your monthly income has a very negative effect on your real life, then there would be a need to control your life patterns a little more. If you think it is hard to donate because it feels like a waste of money, you need to change your mind. This is because if you couldn't get value from the world from the beginning, the money you can have is 'zero', or none. In addition, if you have more true gratitude through repeated donations, a virtuous cycle of positiveness and gratitude is created, and as a result this will grow your own value. So, the amount corresponding to 10% of your income for a donation will gradually increase.

Ideas

The values you accumulate must be provided to and exchanged in the world, and the value must be made into item to do this. It is an idea that makes the value into an item. Therefore, you need to think about a lot of good ideas and this is also a way to grow overall values.

Just as if you use more muscles in your body, your muscles get stronger, if you think about more ideas, you can have more good ideas. In other words, it is to strengthen the muscle of ideas. Specifically, the idea can be about business items. An idea for a business doesn't have to be big or great. When you think of ideas, you can see that some ideas are completely useless and some are practically impossible. And there are also many ideas that already exist in the world. However as you constantly devise and accumulate such small ideas, you can gradually have better ideas, and even ideas that seem useless may be combined and recreated as a great idea. Or some ideas weren't able to be realized at the time they were thought of, but can later be realized through environmental changes such as the development of technology over time. Therefore, it is good to continuously think about ideas without limiting anything.

To create ideas, you need to develop the skill to make values into items. But first of all, there should be a lot of value materials that can be made into items. In other words, accumulating a lot of knowledge and experience as materials would be the foundation to make better ideas. Therefore, accepting as much from the world as possible through all methods such as books, newspapers, seminars, working, business, and investment is the most important and basic way to make good business ideas while having a positive attitude.

You need to record all ideas that come to mind at any time, and you also need to train yourself separately to create ideas. When you think about what happened during the day before going to bed every night in chronological order, some of what happened might be good and some might be bad. At this time, it would be good training to think about how to make the good things better and how to improve bad things, and then think about how to utilize them in a business way. In this way, you can create ideas for one business item for about 15 minutes a day. As such, creating ideas every day will be not only good for business but also help to organize and remember the day and to preserve and grow the values.

CHAPTER 3. DAY SYSTEM

Once again, I would like to say that you need to reduce resistance and utilize inertia well in order to grow the values. Therefore, it's better to create a system that will be operating in a day when you spend the day doing something rather than thinking and making your effort grow into values every moment. If you spend the day according to the system, you can reduce resistance and make good use of inertia. And you can easily repeat it without getting tired or giving up.

There are some factors that you should prepare in advance before creating a daily system. You may need some time to prepare these factors related especially to money among the following factors, so it is necessary to be ready as soon as possible.

- Set a mission

- Set a vision

- Prepare a financial statement (at current status)

- Prayer of gratitude

- Life pattern and self-control that can allow you to live with 60% of your income

A daily system can be created by dividing it into an execution cycle. It would be good to follow the following system as it is or to create your own system by referring to this.

A system to be repeated every day

Division	Time	Tools
Starting routine	05:45-05:46	Making the bed
	05:47-05:52	Morning exercise
	05:55-06:10	Morning diary
	06:10-06:25	Meditation
	06:25-06:55	Goal writing
Accumulating value materials	06:55-07:55	Reading books*
	07:55-08:40	Newspaper
Daily life	09:30-18:00	Work / Investment
Finishing routine	21:45-22:00	Idea
	22:00-22:05	Prayer of gratitude
	22:05-	Meditation

* If there is not enough time due to the labor contract, you can use your commute time. If you use public transportation, you can secure about an hour of reading time a day with about 30 minutes on the way to work and about 30 minutes on the way home. If the environment does not allow you to do this, you should make an hour for reading by making as much time as possible from your daily routine.

A System to be Repeated at Specific Cycles

Cycle	Tools	Description
2 weeks	Writing	Use all the materials including books, newspapers, and seminars for the last 2 weeks, write at least 400 words.
1 month	Seminar	Participate in any topics that interest you, regardless of the field.
	Settle financial statement	Record changes in financial statements over the past month (1 month) and predict and make a plan for next new month.
	Check vision	Check any progress for achieving vision; revise it if necessary.
3 months	Idea review	Review the ideas you've accumulated over three months and update them if there are any ideas to revise or combine together.
	Diary review	Review what thoughts and feelings you've had over past three months and make future plans.
	Writing review	Read the writings you've made so far and organize the values you've accumulated in your thoughts.
1 year	Check mission	Think about whether the mission set before the year has passed is your true mission and revise it if necessary.

* * *

Even if you create a daily system like this, it would still be difficult to execute and form a habit. However, execution and repetition are almost impossible without such systems. It will take about 3 hours a day on average to execute the system. And investing about 3 hours a day for your own happiness will never be too much. In particular, if you place the start of your routine properly, you can easily execute it by using inertia and reduce the time needed to overcome big resistances to less than 1 hour a day on average. In addition, once you form the habit of living according to the system, the resistance would be reduced to a much greater extent.

A daily system is a tool you must follow and maintain throughout your lifetime. In terms of its effect, you can feel the inner changes in around 3-6 months depending on your current status, and there would be realistic changes in your living environment in around 1-2 years, and you will certainly live a happy life close to the completion you have thought of from the beginning in around 5-10 years. If you live according to the above system for 10 years, you will read nearly 1,000 books, create more than 3,000 business items and write more than the equivalent of 1 book in simple calculations. Furthermore, you will live while fulfilling your vision according to your mission with a positive attitude. So, it is natural that there should be noticeable changes and you certainly feel far more happiness in your life. Therefore, you must invest about 3 hours a day for yourself to be rich, have freedom, and live happily.

CHAPTER 4. SMALL LESSONS FOR A GREAT DAY

Once you create a daily system, you can make any day a great day by following the system well. There are concepts and a mindset you must understand to make a great day. They are correct concepts about diligence and laziness and the mindset not to be controlled under perfectionism.

Diligence and Laziness

As you do more valuable work, you may face greater resistance. And diligence is power to overcome resistance. On the other hand, laziness is to choose work with little resistance, which means with low value. Some people perceive diligence the same as the concept of working hard, but you need to distinguish this clearly. You can work hard for things with high value as well as things with low value or almost no value. Therefore, it is good to work hard, but it is much more important to work hard for the valuable and must-do work.

When working at a company, sometimes people work hard on something less important or have enough time to do it, leaving behind what they need to do right away. Or people sometimes read a book rather than doing homework or clean up their desk which they didn't do well rather than studying even during the period for the preparation of exams. Choosing another job without overcoming resistance from the most important work that needs to be done with priority at the moment is laziness, not diligence no matter how hard working it is.

Therefore, you need to recognize exactly whether you spend the day diligently or lazily. In particular, even if the system is made perfectly, if following the system can be the direction of laziness due to a certain circumstance, you should flexibly change the direction of action and move forward toward diligence.

Perfectionism

There is no perfection in what you do. In other words, there is no 100%. No matter how strong of a will you have, you can't do everything perfectly, and even if you complete everything according to your plan, you can't exercise 100% concentration every moment. Therefore, you must always recognize that nothing can be perfect.

If you pursue perfectionism, there will be big problems. They are guilt, frustration, and giving up. If you pursue perfectionism on certain work, you can easily feel frustration even for the smallest crack or mistake and it makes you give up quickly. Even worse, you may feel guilty. If you pursue perfectionism, you may easily give up the daily system if you fail several times with certain circumstances or internal reasons. This is because you may feel frustration or guilt for breaking its perfection. Therefore, if you break away from perfectionism more, a daily system can last for longer and even for a lifetime. However, you shouldn't make the mistake of interpreting "breaking away from perfectionism" as meaning not being perfect. If you can be perfect, of course, it is certainly a good thing. It just means that you shouldn't feel frustration or guilt even when you fail something while trying to create perfection as much as possible.

Keeping a daily system and creating a great day would be enough to be at more than 80%. It means that it is enough to make more than 300 days a year and more than 25 days a month as great days. However, you must be wary to not be generous to yourself by thinking you don't need to keep this for 65 days a year and 5 days a month. If you become generous to yourself, such generosity increases more and it eventually creates a habit of laziness. Basically, you should try to make a great day without skipping even one day and restart the system immediately even if you've temporarily stopped it.

It is same for the other areas. For example, if you pursue the exact proportion and 100% in terms of investment for the asset portfolio and risk management, you may miss a big flow and not be able to make optimal judgments. In conclusion, you must be wary of being immersed in perfectionism in all areas of life and exercise flexibility.

PART V. WRAP-UP

CHAPTER 1.
SUMMARY

I will try to simplify and summarize all of my explanations so far and parts that were not sufficient in this chapter. Please remember the following summaries and try to apply them to your life. Then, your life will be certainly changed in a positive way much faster than you expect.

- The biggest goal in your life is to live happily.
- Freedom and riches must follow happiness.
- You must find a mission, set a vision, and act accordingly to live happily.
- Value is an energy that makes people's minds move in a positive direction.
- Value is a combination of matter and imagination.
- Values of pure matter don't change.
- Values of imagination depreciate, but they can grow continuously with the input of additional imagination.
- You must accept the values from the world as they are in order to grow your own values. And you must

live with gratitude and a positive attitude.

- Luck is an opportunity. You must have a positive attitude and have a wide range of knowledge, experience, and personal connections to obtain luck.
- Work is an exchange of values.
- The three factors of value production are capital, land, and labor, and you must work in all three areas.
- It is labor that exchanges values with money immediately and it is business that exchanges values with money after adding other values.
- It is labor in which income is immediately lost as soon as the value input is stopped, and it is business that can gain income only through the regular input of values.
- You must work for learning and you must finally do business no matter other types of work you started with.
- Investment is to store value in assets.
- Work is to exchange values and investment is to store values. Therefore, work and investment should be done together. The final stage of work is investment.
- You shouldn't consider the numbers shown on money as the amount of value. Money is like a gift card.
- Changes in value and changes in price appear differently. The price of an asset that attracts people's attention increases. Therefore, it is a good investment to buy assets that attract less attention from people while having increased values.

- You should create a portfolio and manage risk to make good investments.
- The proportion of the portfolio composition is 30% basic assets, 35% cash flow assets, 25% value growth assets, and 10% value defense assets based on net assets.
- The asset you must acquire first is the basic asset (accommodation) and you must acquire assets corresponding to about 70 times your monthly income within 3 to 5 years.
- You never sell gold and silver unless the government system has collapsed.
- Risk begins with loans.
- The appropriate level of risk management is 5% self-asset, 20% basic asset, 75% cash flow assets, 20% value growth assets, and 0% value defense assets. You must have cash corresponding to 3-6 times your average monthly expenses.
- Once you've completed the portfolio composition and risk management, you can enjoy investing as if you are playing a game, and understanding the 4 seasons of investment is the key to playing the game well.
- You must make and manage your personal financial statement.
- You must create living patterns that can allow you to live with 60% of your monthly income with the remaining 40% going toward 10% for donation, 10% for saving, and 20% for loan repayment.
- The practical effect of 10% for savings and 20% for

loan repayment is the increased control you gain.
The surplus plays a practical role in investing.

- When you start to acquire assets after starting
economic activities, you must clean up your loans as
quickly as possible by paying back at least 30% of
your monthly income if there are loans. If there are
no loans, you must save at least 30% to acquire a
basic asset as quickly as possible.
- The thing that grows value is execution and it can be
done within a single day, only today.
- To continuously execute, you must make a routine
and properly place it within the day so that the day
can operate like a system.
- A daily system is composed of 'Starting routine
– Work / Investment – Finishing routine'. The value
growth in a day is mostly completed during the
starting routine section.
- You shouldn't be immersed in perfectionism and
shouldn't feel any frustration and guilt for not
executing things as planned. However, more than
80% of all plans should be executed.

CHAPTER 2. SPIRIT AND WORLD

I will finish this book with the explanation of the most powerful energy in the world and laws you must know while living your life. They are the energy of spirituality and the law of trials. This is a part many people emphasize and I also agree with their importance. However it is very difficult to understand its nature and cause-and-effect relationship, so I hope you just accept it with your heart rather than understanding it rationally.

The Energy of Spirituality

There is a God. Regardless of whether you believe in God or not, or how you define its form, it is obvious that there is a God. And humans have spirituality. Spirituality is the only tool to communicate with God. Therefore, the greatest power that moves one's life comes from spirituality. This is because humans communicate with God through spirituality and as a result, God leads your life.

Once again, it is to communicate with God through spirituality. Communication must be made both ways. You must avoid unilateral requests and firm your belief that God will lead you in a good direction if you just devote yourself to pray and believe. You must refine your spirituality so that you can ask for the path, ask for help, and better understand the divine will. When the divine will and what you want to do is consistent and when you move in the direction that God wants, God will help you with what you do better and lead you to your destination. Therefore, you can exercise the greatest power when you find your mission through spirituality and move according to that mission. It is the same for vision and specific goals.

The divine will is already engraved in man's heart. Therefore, listening to and following your true heart is the way to refine spirituality and follow the divine will. If you follow the divine will, that is to follow your true heart, God will guide and help you move in the right direction and create results. It is in the same context as the saying "When you want something, all the universe conspires in helping you to achieve it," from *Alchemist*, a novel by Paulo Coelho. And the results God helped with and created always appear much better than your plans or expectations, and the process is made with miraculous help in an unexpected way. It is like the saying, 'All things work together for good,' in the Bible. This is why people with great success commonly say, "Success comes much faster than I thought," "I was lucky," or "I did nothing. Others helped me a lot with everything."

The Law of Trial

You always encounter trials when achieving certain lofty goals. And as you have bigger goals, the trials become even bigger. This is the law of the world and I refer to it as the law of trial. You must go through the process of trials according to the law of trial to set and complete your vision.

Trials come right before the goal is about to achieved. This is a kind of test or training that sees whether you deserve to have success. No one will be pleased with the process of trials, but you should welcome them rather than being scared or avoiding them. This is because going through trials means success is right in front of you. And you must know that success can collapse at any time if the goal is achieved and succeeds without any trials. So, you must always look forward to the trials. Success without any trials is one that has not yet been completed.